Contents

By matching up the guides at the edge of this page with the marks opposite them along the edge of the book, you can quickly turn to the unit containing the material you want.

COURT REPORTING:

Grammar and Punctuation

Diane Castilaw-Palliser B.A., M.A.

Published by

K61 **SOUTH-WESTERN PUBLISHING CO.**

CINCINNATI   WEST CHICAGO, IL   DALLAS   LIVERMORE, CA

Copyright © 1987
by South-Western Publishing Co.
Cincinnati, Ohio

ISBN: 0-538-11610-2
Library of Congress Catalog Card Number: 86-62133

1 2 3 4 5 6 7 8 D 2 1 0 9 8 7

Printed in the United States of America

Preface

The intent of this text is to serve as a guide to both students of court reporting and working professionals. Accurately recording the exchanges of attorneys and witnesses is an impressive achievement in itself; however, an equally challenging aspect of the job occurs later: transcription. The seasoned court reporter is aware of the questions that can arise in attempting to impose grammatical order upon an oral dictation. The purpose of this book is to assist the court reporter in answering these inevitable questions. Lengthy, sometimes heated debates over hyphenation, commas, rambling run-ons—such time-wasting quandaries can be resolved with quick reference to this book.

Mastery of grammar and punctuation principles and proofreading skills will give the student reporter a distinct advantage when that student enters the work force. As a working reporter, he or she will need to spend far less time debating and deliberating as a result of mastering a significant portion of this text.

While teaching courses to students of court reporting, the author found a void in available literature for the profession. Although there are a handful of books that have been developed exclusively for court reporters, each covers only certain aspects of the job; none is suitable as a single, comprehensive reference. This book should fill that void.

The approach is purely practical. Information has been included on the basis of its usefulness to court reporters, either directly and obviously or as a foundation. Much of the material in traditional grammar texts, such as those used in college English courses, is not contained herein. The reason is simply that the more esoteric aspects of grammar would be of little or no practical use to the court reporter (though, granted, such knowledge could do no harm!). The usefulness of some of the grammar sections may not be apparent immediately, but they were included because they lead to an understanding of the more obviously useful applications, in particular, punctuation.

The text is divided into 12 units, with sections numbered sequentially for quick and easy reference. Unit 1 is a glossary of grammatical and other specialized terms. Moving the glossary from its traditional back-of-book location underscores the importance of being familiar with these basic terms before, not during or after, moving on to the other units. Starting with a glossary also renders unnecessary the defining of terms as they occur in later units. Reviewing the glossary, with particular attention to unfamiliar terms, is the best way to begin to use this book.

Units 2 and 3, on grammar and punctuation, follow the glossary. The need to gain a thorough knowledge of grammar may seem less urgent than learning punctuation; nevertheless, the latter depends heavily on the former. The two are interdependent, and acumen in one but not the other cannot produce a first-rate transcript unless the court reporter is one of those rare individuals with an intuitive "knack" for punctuation.

A court reporter's need for punctuation skills is recognized by all. Speech being far less perfect than written words, the court reporter must depend on punctuation to render a transcript clear to its readers. Punctuation makes it possible for the transcript to reveal what actually occurred during the proceedings. A punctuation error can change the tone or even the meaning of what was said. A reporter's recording accuracy, although certainly crucial, is not sufficient in itself, for it is punctuation that can correctly or incorrectly color and interpret those words.

Units 4 through 8 cover capitalization, numbers, abbreviations, word division, and compounds. Unit 9, Homonyms and Other Confusions, is a dictionary of sorts that defines frequently confused "sound-alikes" and shows their use in sample sentences. Basic suggestions for setting up a transcript are covered in Unit 10. The lack of uniformity of formatting that exists throughout the industry limits the amount of information that could be presented accurately. Yet the information included in this unit provides a pattern that will serve as a valid "jumping-off" point. Included in this unit is a section on proofreading that lists standard symbols and gives examples of how these symbols are to be used. It also offers suggestions for more effective proofreading of one's work.

Unit 11 is devoted to exercises that test for understanding of the principles outlined in previous units. These exercises, as well as the shorter exercises incorporated in Units 2 through 9, are of course particularly designed for the student reporter who is using this book, but practicing reporters may also wish to try them as a way of testing or sharpening their skills. The exercises can be skipped over completely by reporters who do not feel the need for them or who are using this book purely for reference.

The reference list in Unit 12 suggests valuable resources to which the student or reporter may turn. It does not claim to be an all-inclusive list of reference materials, but rather presents a good sampling of what is available.

As much pertinent information as could be compacted between the covers has been included with one goal in mind: to offer, in a single book, a complete "style" manual for the court reporting industry.

1

Glossary

Unlike the usual glossary, this glossary is at the front rather than the back of the book. The reason for this departure from tradition is to encourage the reader to become familiar with basic terms before proceeding to subsequent sections. Understanding these terms before embarking on the units that follow will make the reader's path much smoother. For example, the statement in a later unit that acronyms do not employ periods will not stop the reader who already knows, from studying the glossary, what an acronym is. Of course, the glossary is always available for quick reference as necessary.

Whereas this glossary is by no means a complete glossary of grammatical terms—it does not attempt to be—it will provide the court reporter (CR) with a vocabulary quite sufficient for the purposes of this profession. The CR generally does not wish to know grammar for its own sake, but rather for purposes of applying it to the craft of court reporting. The terms have been selected with the CR in mind, as an aid in improving the accuracy and clarity of transcripts.

As you go through this glossary, see how many of the terms you know already. Study the ones you do not know, familiarize yourself with them, and then go on to the other units with that knowledge in hand. Check back whenever you need to.

1   **Academic Degrees**

Degrees earned from colleges and universities. If the degree is abbreviated, periods should be used. Consult an abbreviations dictionary for specialized and foreign degrees.

> Ph.D. (Philosophiae Doctor/Doctor of Philosophy)
> J.D. (Juris Doctor/Doctor of Law)
> D.D.S. (Doctor of Dental Surgery)
> L.H.D. (Litterarum Humaniorum Doctor/Doctor of Humanities)
> B.A. (Bachelor of Arts)
> B.S. (Bachelor of Science)

2   Academic Titles

Positions within academia. Capitals are used when academic titles are accompanied by the person's name but lowercased otherwise. Do not abbreviate academic titles within a transcript.

> I had an appointment to see **Professor Winston** that after-noon, but I ran into **Dean of Sciences Perez** and talked to her at length.
> The **department head**'s office was next to mine.
> I did not particularly like my mathematics **professor**.
> Mary Wentworth, my English **professor**, studied under **Chairman Ebert** at Rutgers.

3   Acronym

An abbreviation that forms a new "word" from the first letter or two of a series of words that together make up a term. No periods are used after the letters. Acronyms often are thought of as being words in and of themselves to the extent that they are sometimes not recognized as being abbreviations. Some are written uppercased, and others are not. Consult your dictionary.

> ALCOA (Aluminum Company of America)
> Amtrak (American travel by track)
> BASIC (Beginner's All-Purpose Symbolic Instruction Code)
> CAM (Content Addressable Memory)
> Conrail (Consolidated Rail Corporation)
> HUD (Housing and Urban Development)
> NASA (National Aeronautics and Space Administration)
> NATO (North Atlantic Treaty Organization)
> radar (radio detecting and ranging)
> RAM (Random Access Memory)
> SAGE (Semi-Automatic Ground Environment)
> scuba (self-contained underwater breathing apparatus)
> snafu (situation normal, all fouled up)

4   Active Voice. *See* Voice

5   Adjective

One of the eight parts of speech. An adjective modifies, qualifies, limits, defines, or describes a noun or a pronoun. There are several types of adjectives (proper, descriptive, possessive, articles, demonstrative) and three degrees of adjectives of comparison (positive, comparative, and superlative).

We took **a long, leisurely, satisfying** lunch.

Upon receiving **the five wilted** roses, **her pleasant** mood changed.

The longer skirt made **a prettier** ensemble, in **my humble** but **honest** opinion.

6   **Adverb**

One of the eight parts of speech. Like an adjective, an adverb modifies; but it modifies a verb, an adjective, or another adverb. It may also modify an entire sentence, clause, or phrase. Adverbs tell how, when, where, to what extent, etc., something was done. Many, though not all, adverbs are formed by adding the suffix *ly* to an adjective.

I couldn't walk **straight**, so I held onto the rail **desperately**.

Certainly Ms. Deville spoke **courteously** to me.

7   **Ampersand (&)**

A character that stands for the word *and*. The CR should use the ampersand only for company names in which it is normally used. Do not ever use the ampersand to mean *and* except in those cases.

Wills, Thiessen, Chang **&** Bates represented the plaintiff.

Charles Ellington **&** Sons is the plaintiff in this action.

Ralph Warren **and** Sons, Inc., was established 30 years ago.

8   **Antecedent**

Literally, that which precedes or goes before; specifically, the word or words to which a pronoun refers. A pronoun and its antecedent must agree in number and person.

When **Jim** called, he asked my **parents** if they would be going to his party next week. (*Jim* is the antecedent of *he*; *parents* is the antecedent of *they*.)

I just asked if **either** of the boys had lost his book. (*Either* is the antecedent of *his*.)

9   **Antonyms**

Words with opposite meanings.

lazy • industrious   attractive • repellent
kind • cruel

10 **Appositive**

A substitute name or "renamer" that is placed beside a noun or a pronoun to explain or identify it.

> One of my cousins, **Rick Davidson**, rode in the car with me.
> I read all of author **James Michener**'s books.
> My favorite author, **Susan Howatch**, was unknown to William.

11 **Article**

A word used as an adjective to indicate the degree of definiteness. The definite article is *the*; the indefinite articles are *a* and *an*.

> I wanted to see **a** movie with **an** ending that was happy.
> I saw **the** movie at 8:00 p.m.

12 **Auxiliary Verb**

A verb used along with the main verb to show person, number, mood, tense, or voice. The 23 most common auxiliary verbs are *is, am, are, was, were, have, has, had, be, been, being, do, did, shall, will, can, may, might, must, could, should, would,* and *does.* Auxiliary verbs are also called helping verbs.

> I **will** try to remember exactly what happened.
> I **can** recall it clearly.

13 **Caret ( )**

A proofreading symbol that indicates where something should be inserted.

>   **exactly**
> I should have told him ∧where I was going.

14 **Case**

The form of a noun or pronoun that shows the relationship of that word to other words in the sentence. A word's case depends on its function in the sentence. There are three cases: nominative, objective, and possessive. *See individual entries.*

15 **Cedilla**

A hooked mark placed under the letter *c* to indicate that it should be pronounced like an *s.* On the typewriter, a cedilla can be made by typing a comma beneath the letter.

> façade
> garçon

16   **Clause**

A group of related words that contains both a subject and a verb. A clause can be independent or dependent (subordinate). *See individual entries.*

> Harrison handed me the book from the top shelf.
>   (independent)
> When Harrison handed me the book from the top shelf,
>   (dependent)

17   **Clipped Form**

A shortened version of a word, used in conversational or informal language. No periods are used with clipped forms.

> *math* for *mathematics*   *gym* for *gymnasium*
> *pro* for *professional*   *flu* for *influenza*
> *ad* for *advertisement*

18   **Colloquial**

Having to do with conversation. Colloquial language, though not technically incorrect, is generally unacceptable for formal writing. CRs cannot avoid using colloquial language when they are transcribing questions and answers, but it should be edited out of judges' and attorneys' lines.

> Come on, man, let's get out of here.

19   **Colloquy**

An on-the-record dialogue, usually between attorneys but sometimes involving witnesses, most often having to do with the discovery process, particularly the issue of whether or not the questioning attorney has violated its parameters. Colloquy is often a vehicle for discussing whether the judge should make a ruling on this question. The format differs from the format for Q & A (question/answer).

20   **Comma Splice**

The punctuation error of using a comma between two independent clauses that are not connected by a coordinating conjunction. *See also* **Run-on Sentence**

> I saw him running from the office, I tried to catch him.
> We telephoned Juan at his home, no one answered.

21 Comparative Degree

The form of a descriptive adjective used to express a comparison between two persons or things. It is usually formed by adding *er* to the adjective or using the word *more*.

more difficult   worse (an irregular form)
more careful   sweeter
hotter   better (irregular)

22 Complex Sentence

A sentence having one independent clause and one or more dependent clauses.

Whatever he was doing to our truck, he did not have our permission to do so.
Unless I misunderstood, Andre told her that he was resigning.

23 Compound Sentence

A sentence having at least two independent clauses.

We planned to meet that night, but he didn't show up.
Maria sat down at the table, she began to stare at him, and then she suddenly started screaming and ranting.

24 Compound Word

A combination of two or more closely associated words that constitute a single entity. Some compound words are written open, some are hyphenated, and some are written solid.

high school (open)   notebook (solid)
self-imposed (hyphenated)

25 Compound-Complex Sentence

A sentence having two or more independent and one or more dependent clauses.

Whenever we saw Mr. Chevetta, he refused to speak to us, but we just figured he was an eccentric, a loner, and we didn't get angry about it.

26 Conjunction

One of the eight parts of speech. The word comes from the Latin word for "joining together." Conjunctions act as connectives. There are three types of conjunctions: coordinating, subordinating, and correlatives. *See individual entries.*

> I will **either** give it away **or** sell it.
> Terri **and** Bryan **and** Mel were down at the river; **so** I decided to go down there **and** join them.

27   Conjunctive Adverb

An adverb that acts as both adverb and conjunction. A conjunctive adverb, followed by a comma, usually comes between related independent clauses that are separated by a semicolon or a period. Examples: *also, anyway, besides, consequently, finally, furthermore, hence, however, incidentally, indeed, instead, likewise, meanwhile, moreover, nevertheless, next, nonetheless, otherwise, still, then, therefore, thus.*

> I didn't want to see him that night. **Moreover,** I don't ever want to see him again.
> She didn't repay the loan; **incidentally,** that wasn't the first time it had happened.

28   Coordinating Conjunction

A conjunction that connects parts of equal rank. The coordinating conjunctions include *and, or, but, nor, yet,* and *for.*

> Across the river **and** over the hill we ran. (connects two phrases)
> Neither he **nor** I understood what was happening. (connects two pronouns)
> Call Mrs. Lopez **or** write a letter to the head of the department. (connects two clauses)

29   Correlatives

Connectives, or conjunctions, that are used in pairs but are not adjacent to one another. Some of the most common correlatives are *either . . . or, neither . . . nor, not only . . . but also, both . . . and,* and *whether . . . or.*

> I was going to **either** call him **or** write him a letter, but I put it off until it was too late.
> **Neither** Mr. Tiller **nor** Mrs. Wiley attended the board meeting.
> **Whether** he decided to stay **or** go made no difference to me.

30 **Declarative Sentence**

A sentence that makes a statement and ends with a period.

> There was no one in the house with me.
> We couldn't understand a word he said.

31 **Definite Article.** *See* **Article**

32 **Demonstrative Pronoun**

A pronoun that acts as a "pointer": *this, that, these,* or *those.* Demonstrative pronouns act as adjectives when paired with a noun (*this house, these children*).

> **This** was my idea; yours wasn't as good.
> **These** are not my gloves; **those** are mine.
> I have never seen **that** happen here before.

33 **Dependent Clause**

A clause that cannot stand alone as a sentence, even though it has a subject and a verb. Also called a subordinate clause. *See also* **Independent Clause**

> While he was away
> Before we left town
> Because of all the problems the family had

34 **Descriptive Adjective**

An adjective that describes a noun or pronoun. A descriptive adjective will be in one of three degrees: positive, comparative, or superlative. *See individual entries for degrees.*

> pretty   clever
> violet   more selfish

35 **Direct Address**

Word(s) representing the person, thing, or group to whom one is speaking.

> **Susan,** summon the magistrate.
> **Jan and Mary,** you are both exaggerating.
> **Members of the jury,** you have received your
>   instructions.

36 Direct Object

The word or words denoting the thing or person that receives the action of the verb. To find the direct object, first find the subject and the verb and then ask "whom?" or "what?" The verb must be in the active voice to have a direct object. *See also* **Indirect Object**

> Jose watched the **game** with us.
> I gave Timothy a **gift** because he was leaving the next day.
> The child hit the **cat**.

37 Direct Quotation

Quotation of words *exactly* as they were spoken or written. A direct quotation is set off with quotation marks.

> John Samuels said to me, and I quote, "Mrs. Alvarez, you must leave the house immediately."
> He wrote in his letter of 30 June, and I read from that letter, "You will regret these actions, and I will make sure that you do."

38 Ellipsis Mark

A mark (. . .) indicating the omission of words, sentences, or even paragraphs within quoted material. The CR will not need to use an ellipsis mark unless, while reading quoted matter, the reader says, "Dot dot dot" to indicate an ellipsis. Do not use this mark to show an interruption, pause, or dropping off of speech.

39 Elliptical Construction

An omission of a word or words that does not obscure the meaning of the sentence.

> His appearance was normal but his voice strange. (*was* has been omitted after *voice*)
> I am a faster and better typist than she. (*is* has been omitted after *she*)
> However accomplished, the job must be complete by tomorrow. (*it is* has been omitted after *however*)

40 Enumeration

A list, set up formally and indented from the body of the text.

> The following have been proved today:
>
> 1. The defendant was present when Mr. McRae died.

2. The defendant did nothing to help Mr. McRae.
3. The defendant could have assisted Mr. McRae and possibly saved his life.

41   Expletive

- An exclamatory word or phrase, especially a "four-letter word" or obscenity, usually followed by an exclamation mark.

  Dammit! How many times are you going to ask me that question!

- A filler, usually "it" or "there," that fills some kind of space but does not add to or change the meaning of the sentence.

  Try harder to make **it** understood what you mean.
  There were several boys standing around on the corner that night.

42   Fragment

A phrase or clause written as though it were a complete sentence although it is not complete.

  Working early in the morning, trying to get the task done.
  To joke with the woman in the lobby.
  While the plane landed.
  Stella's brother, who lives in Ohio.

43   Function

The "role" a word plays in a sentence; for example, whether it is the subject of a sentence, the direct object, the object of a preposition, and so on.

44   Genitive Case. *See* **Possessive Case**

45   Gerund

A verbal that acts as a noun and is an *ing* form of a verb.

  Talking too much always got her into trouble.
  Thank you for **calling** us.

46   Homographs

Words with the same spelling but different meaning and pronunciation.

  bow and arrow • **bow** your head in prayer
  conduct the orchestra • poor grades in **conduct**

47 **Homonyms**

Words that have the same pronunciation but differ in origin, meaning, and spelling.

> bear/bare   isle/aisle
> hair/hare

48 **Imperative**

A command or a request. Even when expressed in question form, an imperative ends with a period.

> Would you please take a seat.
> Come here, John.

49 **Indefinite Article.** *See* **Article**

50 **Indefinite Pronoun**

A pronoun used to replace a nonspecific group. The indefinite pronouns include *all, each, several, most, many, few, someone, anybody, some, another, neither,* and *either.*

51 **Independent Clause**

A clause that can stand alone as a complete sentence. It contains both subject and verb. *See also* **Sentence**

> We walked to town along the West Hill Road.
> Sometimes the family went for long drives on Sunday afternoons.

52 **Indirect Object**

The word or words denoting the person or thing to which something is given or for which something is done. It is found in a sentence by using this formula: subject + verb + direct object; then ask "to whom?" or "to what?" The answer will be the indirect object.

> I gave **Donald** a book for Christmas.
> Ms. Adamson told **Janice** the truth that day.

53 **Infinitive**

A verbal that usually (though not always) functions as a noun. An infinitive comprises the word *to* and a verb in its present tense.

> **To graduate** was my immediate goal.
> We expected **to move** in December.
> I wanted only **to talk** to him.

54   **Intensive Pronoun**

A "self" pronoun used for emphasis. *See also* **Reflexive Pronoun**

> I **myself** handled the travel arrangements.
> Mrs. Ellis **herself** appeared at the door, not the butler.

55   **Interjection**

One of the eight parts of speech, used to express emotion. An interjection is followed by a comma if mild in tone or by an exclamation point if expressing strong feeling. *See also* **Expletive**

> **Oh,** I think I understand now.
> **Wow!** This is fantastic!

56   **Interrogative Pronoun**

A pronoun used to ask a question: *who, whom, which, what, whose.*

> **Whose** ring did you find on the floor?
> **Which** desk belongs to you?

57   **Interrogative Sentence**

A question.

> Do you recall the night of June 15?
> Where were you that night?

58   **Inversion**

A change in normal word order, usually the placement of a verb before its subject.

> Round and round goes the carousel. (The carousel goes round and round.)
> Down Lake Road and hidden among the trees stands our cabin. (Our cabin stands down Lake Road and hidden among the trees.)

59   **Irregular Plural**

A plural form that does not follow the usual pattern. When in doubt, consult the dictionary.

> child/children   tooth/teeth
> deer/deer   ox/oxen

60   **Jargon**

(1) Highly technical terminology of a certain profession or group, or (2) confused language that does not make sense.

CCDs are not random access; instead, they are serial storage and cycle data through read points to access the stored information.

The releasee, releasee's heirs, executors, administrators, successors, and assigns from all actions, causes of action, suits, debts, dues, sums of money, specialties, covenants, variances, promises, judgments, extents, executions, claims, and demands whatsoever in law, admiralty, or equity which against the releasee . . .

In case of a formulating incident profusing our sense, we can obfuscate reworking or rejuvenation by preventing the termination — conceivably.

61   Jury Charge

Judge's instructions to the jury regarding the laws applicable to the case at hand.

62   Lowercase

Small letters as opposed to capitals (uppercase).

63   Main Clause

An independent clause. It can stand alone as a complete sentence, but it may have attached to it other main clauses, dependent clauses, phrases, or parentheticals.

> Although we were exhausted, **we climbed** to the top of the mountain by using all the strength we had and by refusing to give in to our fatigue, believe it or not.

64   Modifier. *See* **Adjective; Adverb**

65   Modifier, Sentence

A word that modifies the entire sentence.

> **Unfortunately**, we couldn't help her.
> **Certainly** we tried our best.

66   Nominative Case

The form of a pronoun that is used for a subject, a predicate nominative, or an appositive of the subject. Also known as the subjective case. *See also* **Case**

I thought that **she** was the best candidate. (subjects)

It was **he** I wanted to speak to that day. (predicate nominative)

The most productive team, Josef and **I**, should be in charge. (appositive)

67   **Nonrestrictive Element**

A sentence element that is not essential to the meaning. It adds information to the sentence but does not change its meaning. A nonrestrictive element should be set off with commas or dashes. *See also* **Parenthetical Element; Restrictive Element**

Timothy O'Mara, **a man I met only twice in my entire life**, was known to me by reputation.

The teacher of the course, **who was hired last month**, is doing an excellent job.

68   **Noun**

The name of a person, place, thing, idea, or concept. Nouns can be proper (*Ohio, Miss Parker, Union High School*) or common (*state, teacher, school*); collective (*team, choir, orchestra*); abstract (*hatred, envy*) or concrete (*floor, coins, door*).

69   **Object of a Preposition**

A word or group of words that the preposition is relating to another part of the sentence. *See also* **Prepositional Phrase**

In my **opinion**, the estimates of the land's **value** were too low.

After **today** Mr. Carpenter will speak for **us**.

I'm sure that I put it on the **table**, but I found it under the **sofa**.

70   **Objective Case**

The form of a word that is used for a direct object, object of a preposition, appositive of a direct object, object of a verbal, or indirect object.

Will you go to the movie with **us**? (object of preposition)

Give **him** your report when it is finished. (indirect object)

71   **Ordinal**

A number designating place or sequence—first, second, third, etc.

The **25th** day of each month is the day our reports are sent out.

The **fifth** child was a girl—their only daughter.

For the **hundredth** time, I tell you I do not know.

72   **Parenthetical Element**

A nonessential word, phrase, or clause set off by commas or dashes. CRs should never set off parentheticals in parentheses. *See also* **Nonrestrictive Element**

> What you are saying, **in other words,** is that you aren't sure.
>
> I know he was there—**you can't convince me otherwise**—that night and saw everything that happened.

73   **Parts of Speech**

The classification of words according to the function they perform in a sentence. The eight parts of speech are nouns, pronouns, verbs, adjectives, adverbs, prepositions, conjunctions, and interjections. *See individual entries.*

74   **Person**

A term used to indicate whether one is the speaker (first person), is being spoken to (second person), or is being spoken about (third person). "Person" affects the form of verbs and personal pronouns.

> **I** hope things will improve. (first person)
>
> **You** are the first to arrive. (second person)
>
> Mrs. Tell and **she** left on **their** trip last night. (third person).

75   **Personal Pronoun**

A pronoun used to replace a specific noun: *I, my, mine, me, we, our, ours, us, you, your, yours, he, his, him, she, her, hers, they, their, theirs, them, it, its.*

76   **Phrase**

A group of related words that may contain either a verb or a subject, but not both. A phrase cannot stand alone as a sentence. There are several kinds of phrases. The CR need not learn to label all the kinds of phrases but should know the difference between phrases and clauses.

> On the side of the road
>
> Having finished his report
>
> To understand him fully

77   **Positive Degree**

The form of a descriptive adjective that involves no comparison; the basic form that has no characteristic ending. *See also* **Comparative Degree; Superlative Degree**

rusty   kind
soft   easy

78   **Possessive Case**

The form of a word used to show ownership or a similar relationship.

Your car is new, but **mine** isn't.
Our case, though strong, may not seem valid to the judge.

79   **Predicate Adjective**

A complement that acts to modify or describe the subject of the sentence.

Carlos felt **tired** all day.
Sheila seemed **bored** by the discussion.
I am **certain** he told the truth.

80   **Predicate Nominative**

A complement that renames the subject, usually after a form of the verb *to be*, and not placed beside the subject as an appositive is.

Miss Peterson will be the organization's next **president**.
That boy is a real **scoundrel**.

81   **Prefix**

One or more letters placed in front of a root word or stem to change the meaning of the root.

anteroom   **pseudo**intellectual
biweekly   **super**human
reorganization

82   **Preposition**

One of the eight parts of speech. A preposition shows the relationship between a noun or pronoun (the object of the preposition) and another element in the sentence. *See also* **Object of a Preposition; Prepositional Phrase**

We worked **around** the house **for** a few hours.
Jean discovered the money **under** a brick **in** the cellar.

83   **Prepositional Phrase**

A preposition, its object, and any modifiers.

around the house
for a long time
under the kitchen table
after the second traffic light

84   **Pronoun**

One of the eight parts of speech. A pronoun is a word that takes the place of a noun. Pronouns may be classified as personal, indefinite, relative, interrogative, intensive, reflexive, or demonstrative. *See individual entries.*

85   **Proper Noun.** *See* **Noun**

86   **Reflexive Pronoun**

A "self" pronoun that refers to its antecedent. *See also* **Intensive Pronoun**

Joe hurt **himself** with that knife.
We did **ourselves** an injustice.

87   **Relative Pronoun**

A pronoun that introduces a dependent clause.

The boy **who** spoke to you was my cousin.
Whoever comes to my house first will help me prepare.
The house **that** we bought had a swimming pool.

88   **Restrictive Element**

An element that is essential to the meaning of a sentence. Omitting it would alter or obscure the meaning of the sentence. *See also* **Nonrestrictive Element**

The money **that I lost** was Mary's savings.
The child **who wins the contest** will appear on television.

89   **Root**

The base of a word to which prefixes and suffixes may be added to change or qualify the meaning of the original root.

rephrase   **im**perfect
overestimate   **bi**monthly

90   Run-on Sentence

Two sentences improperly written as one. Run-on sentences are of two kinds: fused or comma splice. A fused sentence is one without any punctuation between the two sentences. A comma splice uses a comma instead of a period or semicolon to separate two independent clauses.

> The man ranted on for the better part of two hours finally
> the microphone shorted out. (fused)
> She drove for hours hoping to find medical help, instead
> she found only out-of-order phones. (comma splice)

91   Salutation

A greeting.

> Ladies and Gentlemen of the Jury:
> Your Honor,
> Madam,

92   Sentence

A complete thought that contains both a subject and a verb and can stand alone (an independent clause). Sentences can be grouped according to their structure (simple, compound, complex, compound-complex) or by their "tone" or content (declarative, imperative, interrogative, exclamatory). *See individual entries.*

93   Serial Comma

The final comma before the conjunction in a series or list. The CR should not omit this comma unless the final items constitute a unit.

> We purchased nails, boards, and a hammer.
> The lunch consisted of salad, bread, and red beans and
> rice. (*red beans and rice* is one dish: no comma)
> She wanted to decorate the room in beige, pine green,
> rust, and dark brown.

94   Series

Words, phrases, or clauses listed and separated by commas, semicolons, or conjunctions. *See also* **Enumeration**

> Nonetheless, I consulted my attorney, Ms. Perkins; had her
> look over the plans, advise me, and make changes; and I
> then embarked, though carefully.
> We searched in the office, under all the desks, in the
> drawers, and on the shelves.

I invited Sara and Jamie and Marta and you.
I bought a radio, a toaster, a blender, and a microwave
oven.

95   Simple Sentence

A sentence consisting of one independent clause; either the subject or
the verb may be compound, however.

His team won the meet that night.
Joyce was supposed to buy the hot dogs and take them to
the picnic.
Susan and David plotted and printed the route.

96   Slang

Nonstandard, informal language.

He ain't a bum.
I busted my leg all up.

97   Slash. *See* **Virgule**

98   Subject

The person or thing talked about in a sentence or clause.

John called last night.
A good **impression** is important to me.

99   Subjective Case. *See* **Nominative Case**

100   Subordinate Clause. *See* **Dependent Clause**

101   Subordinating Conjunction

A conjunction that connects a subordinate clause with the main clause.
When a subordinating conjunction is placed at the beginning of an
independent clause, the clause is rendered dependent, or subordinate.
Subordinating conjunctions include the following words: *although, after,
unless, until, while, where, whereas, when, whenever, if, before, as, as if,
as though, because, before,* and *wherever.*

Wherever I went, I kept in touch with Jorge.
I will tell you about that **after** I explain one essential
matter.

102 Suffix

Syllable(s) added to the end of a root or root word to change or qualify the meaning of the root.

play**ing**   care**less**
jump**ed**   care**fully**

103 Superlative Degree

The form of a descriptive adjective used to compare three or more persons or things or objects. The superlative is usually formed by adding *est* to the end of the word or using the word *most*.

rudest   most disagreeable
kindest   most considerate
worst (an irregular form) most unsatisfactory

104 Synonyms

Words that have the same or nearly the same meaning.

insane • mad   lukewarm • tepid
jovial • cheerful

105 Tense

The form of a verb that indicates the time of the action. The tenses are the present, past, future, present perfect, past perfect, and future perfect.

He **will investigate** your complaint. (future)
They **asked** Miss Tephra to telephone their home that
   night. (past)
He **will have completed** the report by Monday morning.
   (future perfect)

106 Umlaut

A diacritical mark placed over a vowel, common in German words, to indicate a change in the way the vowel is to be pronounced.

Häushen
natürlichen

107 Uppercase

Capital letters as opposed to small (lowercase) letters.

108 **Verb**

One of the eight parts of speech and one of the two basic, essential elements that make up a sentence. Verbs show action, state of being, or occurrence.

> I **saw** Bill Tomasin **hit** Mr. Davis in the stomach.
> Ralph **was** my secretary for six years, and he **worked** hard.

109 **Verbal**

A form derived from a verb that functions as a noun, adjective, or adverb.

> The **playing** children heard nothing but their own laughter.
> **To play** cards bored me, so I left the room.

110 **Virgule (/)**

A short diagonal line used between two equivalent words, in dates or fractions, to express "per," etc. A virgule is also used to separate lines of poetry when they are written paragraph style rather than line for line.

> and/or   feet/second
> 5/18/82

111 **Voice**

A characteristic of verbs indicating whether the subject does the action (active voice) or the action is done to the subject (passive voice).

> Mrs. Simmons asked Greg Mendes to recite the poem. (active)
> Greg Mendes was asked by Mrs. Simmons to recite the poem. (passive)

2

Grammar

This unit delves into the rules and concepts of grammar, although in a somewhat limited way. A grammarian would find this treatment incomplete, at least from a theoretical viewpoint, but it is complete for the CR's needs. An effort has been made to omit any material that is not of value to a CR, either directly or indirectly as foundational knowledge. The aim is nothing less than producing excellent transcripts, with increased ease and decreased investment of time. No doubt some parts of this unit will require concentration in unfamiliar areas; other parts will be familiar and can be skimmed. We shall begin with the most basic concept of grammar: the sentence.

The Sentence

112   What makes a group of words a sentence? A sentence is a complete thought, a complete statement. Granted, a CR will not be able to eliminate all nonsentences from transcripts. People do not talk in perfect sentences; however, the CR should make an effort to avoid sentence fragments and run-ons *whenever possible*—and it often is possible—in the witness's words. Furthermore, the CR should see to it that no fragments or run-ons are included in the words of the judges or the attorneys.

Groups of words that are written as a sentence can be classified as one of the following: correct sentence, fragment, or run-on. A fragment can be thought of as "not enough" to constitute a sentence; a run-on can be regarded as "too much" to be a single sentence.

The minimum requirement for a group of words to be classed as a sentence is that it must have a subject and a verb. First search for the verb, which may show action, state of being, or occurrence. Remember to watch for auxiliary verbs.

Jan and Jacob **ate** lunch together every day that month.
Ms. Ardley **seemed** nervous to me and to Jan also.

We **felt** anxious for the report's completion.

They **were trying** their best to please the supervisor.

Benjamin **had given** us a hard time.

After finding the verb, ask who or what did or felt the verb. In the above examples, the first verb is *ate*. Ask who or what ate. The answer is *Jan* and *Jacob*. The subjects of the other sentences are *Ms. Ardley*, *We*, *They*, and *Benjamin*.

Sometimes the subject is understood rather than actually contained in the sentence. In the following examples, the subject is *you* by implication.

Bring me that photo, please.

Compare the two photos, and give me your opinion.

113 **Phrases and Clauses**

In order to have a clear understanding of complete sentences, it is necessary to be able to identify phrases and clauses, and especially to be able to distinguish between them. Both are a group of related words, but there is one crucial difference: a clause has both a subject and a verb.

When he found out the truth

If you make a request

Because you asked for our assistance

The store closed at 9:00 p.m. on that date.

Mr. Henry telephoned us during the early morning hours.

A phrase may have one or the other, but it does not contain *both* a subject and a verb. It may contain neither. There are several kinds of phrases, the most common being the prepositional phrase.

under the oak tree

beneath the armchair

running around the house

To ask too many questions

Thus, it may seem at first that a clause is actually a sentence, as it contains both a subject and a verb. Well, this may or may not be the case.

114 An independent clause is a complete sentence, but a dependent clause, also called a subordinate clause, is not a complete sentence. A dependent clause that is written as though it were a sentence is a fragment. The difference between an independent and dependent clause is simply that a dependent clause has an added feature: a subordinating conjunction at its beginning. Without the subordinating conjunction, the clause would be independent; with it, it is dependent and cannot stand alone as a complete sentence. Table 2-1 lists common subordinating conjunctions.

The following are dependent clauses:

> Until we hear from you
> If you decide to make the purchase
> No matter how hard we try to please Mrs. Timm
> Whoever made the telephone call
> Because nothing was settled
> As soon as we got home

Table 2-1
Subordinating Conjunctions

after	in order that	what
although	in order to	whatever
as	no matter how	when
as if	once	whenever
as soon as	since	where
as though	so that	whereas
because	that	wherever
before	though	while
even if	till	who
for	unless	whoever
if	until	

115 Fragments

A sentence fragment is part of a sentence that is written as though it were a complete sentence. Sometimes the CR can avoid using fragments, but often not. In the examples below, the answers are fragments that could not be avoided.

Q. Where did you find the stuff?
A. Under the bed.

Q. Why did you move the files?
A. Because I was instructed to by Miss Hatchetta.

Q. Where is the grocery where you saw him?
A. Around the corner from my house.

However, in the first example above, if the answer had been longer, the fragment might have been avoided.

Q. Where did you find the stuff?
A. Under the bed, that's where it was.

Avoid

A. Under the bed. That's where it was.

Acceptable

A. Under the bed—that's where it was.

In some instances, however, the fragment cannot be joined logically to the sentence that follows.

Q. Had you met her prior to that day?
A. Perhaps. Janeen had known her a couple of years.

Joining *Perhaps* to the sentence that follows would change the meaning: Perhaps Janeen had known her a couple of years.

Acceptable

A. Perhaps; Janeen had known her a couple of years.

116   Run-Ons

Both comma splices and fused sentences will be called run-ons for the purposes of this text. The CR will have less difficulty avoiding run-ons than fragments. In fact, this common error can be avoided entirely by a skilled CR, and it should not occur at all in transcripts.

Q. What did he say to you?

Correct

A. He told me that he was tired of what had been going on. He was planning to leave.

Acceptable

A. He told me that he was tired of what had been going on; he was planning to leave.

Wrong

A. He told me that he was tired of what had been going on, he was planning to leave.

Correct

Q. I think that you are avoiding the issue, sir. Indeed, you have evaded my questions entirely.

Acceptable

Q. I think that you are avoiding the issue, sir; indeed, you have evaded my questions entirely.

Wrong

Q. I think that you are avoiding the question, sir, indeed, you have evaded my questions entirely.

Correct

Q. Let me ask you one more question. Please answer to the best of your ability.

Acceptable

Q. Let me ask you one more question; please answer to the best of your ability.

Wrong

Q. Let me ask you one more question, please answer to the best of your ability.

One of the most common problems with run-ons involves conjunctive adverbs and transitional phrases. Many CRs tend to use commas where periods or semicolons should be placed. Table 2-2 lists common conjunctive adverbs, and Table 2-3 lists transitional phrases.

Table 2-2
Conjunctive Adverbs

also	incidentally	nonetheless
anyway	indeed	otherwise
besides	instead	still
consequently	likewise	then
finally	meanwhile	therefore
furthermore	moreover	thus
hence	nevertheless	
however	next	

Table 2-3
Transitional Phrases

after all	by the way	in other words
as a result	for example	on the other hand
at any rate	in addition	
at the same time	in fact	

Correct

I asked him to go with us; however, he declined.

Acceptable

I asked him to go with us. However, he declined.

Wrong

I asked him to go with us, however, he declined.

Correct

Sheila was concerned about Mae's getting home safely; therefore, she telephoned Mae's house every 20 minutes.

Acceptable

Sheila was concerned about Mae's getting home safely. Therefore, she telephoned Mae's house every 20 minutes.

Wrong

Sheila was concerned about Mae's getting home safely, therefore, she telephoned Mae's house every 20 minutes.

117   Main Clauses

The main clause of a sentence is the basic clause in the sentence. It may be surrounded by other elements, perhaps several, including phrases, clauses, modifiers, and so on. Often the main clause seems almost hidden by other elements.

MAIN CLAUSE: The children played.

ADD A PHRASE: During the summer evenings the children played.

ADD A CLAUSE: As I recall, during the summer evenings the children played.

ADD SOME OTHER ELEMENTS: Yes, Mr. Werner, as I recall, sometimes during the summer evenings the children played while the adults stayed inside and talked or watched television.

THE MAIN CLAUSE IS STILL THE SAME: The children played.

Classifying Sentences

118   By Content

Sentences may be classified by either their content or their structure. The content of a sentence determines its end punctuation. The following are the types of sentences classified by content:

1. **Declarative Sentence.** This type makes a statement. It declares something to be so or not so. Declarative sentences end with a period.

> The classroom had been vandalized again.
> Some of the clients were taking their business elsewhere.

2. **Imperative Sentence.** This type is a command or a request. It ends with either a period or an exclamation point. Imperatives do not end with question marks.

> Would you please have a seat.
> Tell us your name and address.
> Get out of this room!

3. **Interrogative Sentence.** This is simply a question and of course it ends with a question mark.

> Did you understand all of the questions?
> Shall I repeat what I have said?
> Do you recognize anyone in this room?

4. **Exclamatory Sentence.** This is a sentence that expresses strong emotion. It ends with an exclamation point.

> I can't take this anymore!
> This is ridiculous!
> Mr. Talbot just slapped Nina!

119   **By Structure**

Sentences can be classified according to the way they are set up or written.

1. **Simple Sentence.** A simple sentence is made up of a single independent clause. It may have a compound subject, a compound verb, or both a compound subject and a compound verb; but it contains only one clause.

> Diedre shouted at Matt. (single subject and verb)
> Diedre and Lana shouted at Matt. (compound subject, single verb)
> Diedre shouted at Matt and slapped him. (single subject, compound verb)
> Diedre and Lana shouted and ranted at Matt. (compound subject and verb)

2. **Compound Sentence.** A compound sentence comprises two or more independent clauses.

Wilma walked to town to buy milk, but she didn't
buy it.

I asked you if you wanted to buy the car, and you
told me you didn't want it.

3. **Complex Sentence.** A complex sentence is made up of one independent clause and at least one dependent clause.

When you called, we were asleep.
I left my house after I heard the noises.

4. **Compound-Complex Sentence.** A compound-complex sentence comprises two or more independent clauses and one or more dependent clauses.

If we examine the files, we will find the answers to
the questions and Miss Dies will be able to make
her decision.

You know that Carl saw what happened, and he
told you that he was going to tell everyone after
he got home.

Exercises

A. Identify the following as fragments (F), run-ons (R), or complete sentences (C). Place your answers to the left of the numbers.

1. So that I can better understand what you are trying to say and also so that the members of the jury will have a clear idea about what you are saying.

2. Go.

3. Under the table, on the shelf, around the whole room, as we searched and searched but never found the missing item that Claire needed so desperately to find.

4. We had planned to be there to state our opinion on the matter, however, Jan's accident prevented our attending.

5. We knew where Dad was staying, we had no way of finding Uncle Jonas if we needed him.

6. Everything I knew about his finances and all I could find out.

7. When we were vacationing in Ontario, driving around in our camper, we realized we were lost.

8. To understand how difficult it was for her and to figure out a solution to the problem, knowing that I could never really make things right again.

9. I should have known the minute Ms. Cummings sent you here, although I didn't suspect any underhanded plot myself.

10. We weren't surprised to learn of his demise, moreover, we had been expecting it.

11. Since the time I attended that school, unfortunately, never having graduated.

12. Neither the first nor the last time nor any of the incidents in between—none of them.

13. Unless you come with me.

14. The preference being clear, I made my selection.

15. Because I knew better.

16. We needed the money, therefore, I accepted the offer.

B. In the following sentences, write SC above a subordinating conjunction and CA above a conjunctive adverb.

1. Although I had never gone with them to any conferences, I was invited to go to the Phoenix conference so that I could present the fiscal projections for the next year; therefore, I planned to make that trip whenever it was scheduled.

2. Mother had not seen Mrs. Corriere since 1978, when they were both working in the same company, the place where the explosion seriously injured Mrs. Corriere.

3. As soon as I heard the news I called Maria, whereas when Tomas heard about it, he didn't tell anyone; nevertheless, it wasn't because he didn't care.

4. If you think I did it, say so; however, because you have doubts, I don't think that you will say a word.

5. While we were away, we told him to stay away from the house because the electric fence was turned on; indeed, we warned him about the danger of that fence.

6. Una saw Raphael while he was in Boston, and she said he seemed ill; nonetheless, he seemed fine the next day when Marie talked to him.

7. In order that you might be understood, perhaps you could speak louder so that everyone in this room could hear you whenever you answer the questions.

C. Mark each sentence in two ways: by its content (D = declarative, I = interrogative, IMP = imperative, and EX = exclamatory); and by its structure (S = simple, C = compound, CX = complex, CC = compound-complex). Place your answers to the left of the numbers.

1. Would you please take a seat so that we can begin.

2. Isn't that your signature, and don't you recognize it as being yours?

3. Stop it!

4. Were you in town on the day that he was killed?

5. In other words, as I can recall, I was not near the mill at any given moment that day.

6. Wherever you go and whatever you do, I'll know.

7. I wouldn't have hurt her, and she wouldn't have intentionally hurt me either.

8. I think that he did it, and I am going to prove it.

9. I'm happy with my present position, sir, and wish to remain.

10. Do you expect him to return and, if so, when do you expect him to arrive?

11. Because you wrote the report and because you are responsible for its content, you must present it to the committee and you will have to revise it.

12. Check it out of the library and give it to me.

13. I'm anticipating breaking into that business in a very big way and having tremendous success with it.

14. Are you willing to testify to that, and will you repeat the details to Mr. Kovac?

15. Don't answer that question unless your attorney is present.

Parts of Speech

Nearly all words in the English language can be classified as one of the eight parts of speech: nouns, pronouns, verbs, adjectives, adverbs, prepositions, conjunctions, and interjections. These divisions are made according to a word's function within a sentence as well as the idea or concept it represents. Why does a court reporter need to be able to distinguish among the eight parts of speech? They are the fundamentals of grammar and of proper handling of the English language. An understanding of the eight parts of speech is like fitting together all the pieces in a jigsaw puzzle. Suddenly the whole picture becomes clear. Handling the English language in transcripts becomes a far simpler task when the CR understands this fundamental concept.

Some of the information that follows you may have heard since grammar school. Other parts may be unfamiliar. Go through the entire section, concentrating on those areas where you are weakest.

Nouns

120   The most common definition of a noun is that it names a person, place, or thing. This definition is still a good one, but it may be helpful to add to the definition. Nouns also name someone or something, concepts, ideas, qualities, and animals.

121   **Classifying Nouns**

Nouns are either common or proper. Common nouns name any individual of a specific group, but not a particular member of a group. Proper nouns are specific. Table 2-4 shows the differences between com-

Table 2-4
Common and Proper Nouns

Common	Proper
building	Empire State Building, Chrysler Building, Emerald Street Apartment Building, Fifth District Firehouse, Springfield Police Department
college, university	Goddard College, Tulane University, Illinois State University
book	"The Sound and the Fury," "Tender Is the Night," "A Farewell to Arms"
organization, club	Boy Scouts of America, Future Farmers of America, Knights of Columbus, Business and Professional Women
park	Yellowstone, Great Smoky National Park, William Tell State Park
dog, cat	Garfield, Buffy, Zip, Spot, Minnie
girl	Betty Parkinson, Melissa Rolfe, Patricia Norris
school	Memorial High School, Park Grammar School, Gilbert Junior High
highway, road	Wiggins Lane, Highway 2, Maple Street

mon and proper nouns. For example, *man* is a common noun; *Mr. Evans* is a proper noun. Common nouns are lowercased; proper nouns are uppercased (capitalized).

122   **Collective Nouns**

Collective nouns name a group of words or things that are considered to be a unit. Table 2-5 lists common collective nouns. Collective nouns often present a problem to the CR because it is not always clear whether they take a singular or a plural verb.

> A **herd** of goats is running through Mrs. Zaro's garden.
> A **flock** of geese was screeching noisily overhead.
> The **crew** works 11 hours each day.

All the examples above use a singular verb because the group acted as a single entity. Thus, the collective noun was treated grammatically as a singular subject. Most collective nouns take singular nouns because the group is acting as a unit.

However, there are times when collective nouns take plural verbs. This is done when it is clear that the members of the group are acting individually rather than as a group.

> The group were filling out applications and each would be interviewed.
> The team are tying their shoes with double knots, just as their coach instructed.
> One third of the questions have been answered.

Sometimes this issue is confusing, but remember that most collective nouns behave like singular nouns. In the few cases where the plural

Table 2-5
Common Collective Nouns

army	crowd	herd
audience	duo	jury
band	family	majority
cast	flock	number
choir	fractions:	orchestra
chorus	one fourth	panel
class	one half	percent
committee	seven eighths	platoon
company	two thirds	staff
congregation	gang	team
crew	group	trio

verb is used, the activity under discussion is clearly one that is accomplished individually. When in doubt, use the singular verb.

123 **Concrete and Abstract Nouns**

Another way of classifying nouns is according to whether they represent a tangible (concrete) or an intangible (abstract). Concrete nouns name something that can be perceived by any one of the senses, whereas abstract nouns represent ideas, concepts, or qualities. Table 2-6 lists concrete and abstract nouns.

Table 2-6
Concrete and Abstract Nouns

Concrete	Abstract
wall, floor, house, rug, furniture, mother, sister, brother, father, dog, cat, bricks, plates, trees, shoes, lamp, umbrella, pencil, paper, coat, automobile, school, lawn, store, desk, telephone, television, hat, photograph	love, selfishness, greed, jealousy, envy, contempt, admiration, intelligence, humor, amusement, animosity, awkwardness, fear, anger, cleanliness, ambition, sloth, ambiguity, clarity, curiosity, silliness, shininess, taste

124 **Verbal Nouns**

Verbal nouns look like verbs but behave within a sentence as nouns. Verbal nouns can be a little confusing, but once recognized should cause little or no problem. Gerunds and infinitives are verbals that can act as nouns.

1. **Gerunds.** Gerunds are verbals that end in *ing* and act as nouns within a sentence. Not all words that end with *ing* are gerunds, although they may be nouns; for example, *awning, evening, gelding*.

   > **Running** helps keep Jim fit, but **swimming** is by far his favorite sport. (*Running* and *swimming* both act as the subjects.)
   > He was arrested for **drinking** while **driving.**
   > **Beginning** is the hardest part.
   > After **falling** and **breaking** her foot, Nell called the office for help.

2. **Infinitives.** Another verbal that can act as a noun within a sentence is the infinitive, which consists of the word *to* combined with a verb. However, not every phrase that begins with the word *to* is an infinitive phrase, as *to* can behave as a preposition as well.

> **To understand** was all I wanted. (The infinitive acts as subject.)
>
> He was trying **to cut** the rope. (The infinitive acts as direct object.)
>
> His wish was **to return** to Peru. (The infinitive acts as predicate nominative.)

125   **Nouns and Number**

The term *number* refers to whether a word is singular or plural. The plurals of most nouns are formed by adding the letter *s*.

dog/dogs	play/plays
hair/hairs	basket/baskets
group/groups	

Some plurals are formed by adding *es*.

lunch/lunches	fox/foxes
glass/glasses	wish/wishes

Plurals of most nouns that end with *y* are formed by changing the *y* to *i* and adding *es*.

puppy/puppies	berry/berries
try/tries	salary/salaries

EXCEPTIONS:

monkey/monkeys	turkey/turkeys

Plurals of nouns that end with *f* are sometimes formed by changing the *f* to *v* and adding *s* or *es*.

life/lives	elf/elves
half/halves	shelf/shelves

Some words remain the same, whether in singular or plural form.

deer/deer	sheep/sheep
moose/moose	

Some singular words become a new word in plural form:

ox/oxen	mouse/mice
child/children	woman/women

Musical terms form plurals by adding *s* after the letter *o*.

piano/pianos cello/cellos
solo/solos

Hyphenated compound words form plurals by adding *s* to the main part of the compound.

brother-in-law/brothers-in-law
commander-in-chief/commanders-in-chief

Plurals of abbreviated titles of respect are formed as follows:

Miss/Misses Mrs./Mmes.
Mr./Messrs. Ms./Mses.

Plurals of letters or symbols are formed with *'s* if omitting the apostrophe would cause confusion.

a's o's x's

If there is no possibility of confusion, plurals of numbers, letters, and symbols may be formed without the apostrophe.

1970s (*1970's* is acceptable, though not the preferred style)
ABCs (*ABC's* is acceptable)
Ps and Qs (*P's and Q's* is acceptable)

Note: Use the apostrophe to form the plurals of *A, E, I, O,* and *U. As, Es, Is, Os,* and *Us* are words, or look like words, not like plurals of letters.

The above does not claim to be a complete analysis of plural formation. It is, however, a general guideline that covers many plurals. As usual, when in doubt, consult the dictionary.

Mention should be made of one of the most common errors involving plurals, which is confusing plurals with possessives. For example, family names are frequently written incorrectly, as in the example below.

Wrong

The Smith's live on Oak Drive.

Correct

The Smiths live on Oak Drive.

This error of using the possessive form when the plural form is needed is widespread among the general public. We often see signs on mailboxes or front doors that read: *The Miller's, The Willis's,* etc. They should be written: *The Millers, The Willises.*

Remember that plural refers to number; possessive refers to ownership.

126   Nouns and Ownership

The possessive form of nouns demonstrates ownership or a similar relationship. Most singular possessives are formed by adding 's to the singular noun.

> The boy's books were lost last week, but the school's
> librarian has allowed him to use the library's
> copies.

Plural possessives usually are formed by adding an apostrophe after the *s*.

> The two boys' books were lost last week, but their
> teachers' assignments have been short.

There are exceptions. If a singular word already ends with *s*, use just the apostrophe or the 's. Some texts advise that the 's should be added if it is pronounced.

> James's horse OR James' horse

If a plural noun does not end with *s*, treat it as though it were a singular noun by adding 's.

> children's playground   deer's tracks
> men's room

127   Joint/Individual Ownership

Probably the most troublesome aspect of possessive nouns is when two or more are used together. The rule is this: for joint ownership, make only the second (or last) noun possessive; for individual ownership, both (or all) should be made possessive.

> Mary's and Fran's dresses (unlikely that Mary and Fran
>   would own a single dress jointly)
> Mary and Fran's car (if they owned a single car together)
> Chung and Kim's restaurant (if they owned a restaurant
>   jointly)
> Chung's and Kim's restaurants (if they each owned a sepa-
>   rate restaurant)

Sometimes logic will tell you whether ownership is joint or individual.

> Tomas's and Mel's toothbrushes (not something anyone
>   would want to share)

In less obvious cases, the content of the transcript should reveal whether the object or objects are owned individually or jointly.

A relationship similar to ownership, though not exactly the same, employs the possessive form. Examples include such relationships as three months' pay, money's worth, and car's cost.

Exercises

A. Underline all of the nouns in the following paragraph.

Mr. Marsh opened a small grocery on the corner of our block, and he and his wife worked in it. The woman was always in the store — from early morning until late at night. The kids in our neighborhood frequented the store, mostly for gum, candy, or soda. To see the store without Mrs. Marsh was an oddity. Working in the business seemed to agree with Sara Marsh. Her disposition was always pleasant. Garick Marsh, however, liked fishing, hunting, and relaxing around the house. Morris Latham, Garick's buddy, said he knew what would happen in that situation. Garick, filled with restlessness, boredom, and longing, would search for excuses to leave the store. To see Sara Marsh in the store doing all the hauling, pricing, and stacking was a sad sight. It was a disgrace. Refusing to close down the store was Sara's right, her choice; but she needed a helper. Being so determined was a strain on the woman. Anxiety and fatigue showed in her face. Garick spent less and less time there. Garick's idea of fulfillment was to waste time. Sara had the right to take action. She was a woman, not a machine. Ben McGuire saw Sara's dilemma. He helped her, and Garick felt no jealousy, no distrust, no concern.

B. Which nouns in the paragraph are abstract?

C. Which are verbal nouns?

D. Collective Nouns. Select and underline the correct verb in each of the following sentences.

1. One fourth of the students (was, were) selected to take the trip.

2. The cast (selects, select) their own costumes for the play.

3. The herd (was, were) stampeding across his fields.

4. A mob (has, have) gathered outside the embassy.

5. The orchestra (was, were) playing beautifully that night.

6. The team (was, were) trying on uniforms this afternoon.

7. The class (has, have) selected officers for the year.

8. The committee (is, are) being interviewed by the reporter separately and behind closed doors.

9. The gang (is, are) back together again.

10. The family (is, are) moving to Iowa.

E. Write first the plural and then the possessive of each of the following words.

	Plural	Possessive
1. Tom		
2. clown		
3. ax		
4. clutch		
5. chairman		
6. Mr. Smith		
7. alcohol		
8. time		
9. letter		
10. James		
11. kid		
12. lady		
13. Jack		
14. Mr. Thomas		
15. Mrs. Lemmen		

F. Correct any errors in plural or possessive nouns in the following paragraph:

Mr. Weiner's garden was growing well until Jessies' dog got into the gardens petunias. Jessie had a bad habit of letting his dog's run loose into others yards'. Mr. Weiners' insistence that Jessie pay for the seed's as well as two weeks' worth of planting and hard work in the suns' bright heat fell on deaf ear's. Jessie refused to give Mr. Weiner a pennies' worth of compensation. The womens garden club got into the argument when Mr. Weiner's two sister-in-laws saw the damages' done to their relatives effort's. These two formidable female's contacted most of the member's of the lady's auxiliary, and they actually marched in front of Jessies house. Of course, Jessie's family, the McBee's, were horrified. Mrs. McBee had ten years' experience as an attorney, so she knew what her families rights were or weren't. Jessie's brothers, Bob and Jake, weren't at home that day. The womens' signs said: The ABCs of Americas heritage are property, agriculture, and respect. "What's the meaning of such word's?" Jessie shouted. Mrs. Pfister and Mrs. Jacoby's fists were raised. Jessie then brought out two of his dogs' and asked the lady's whether the animal's should be hanged or imprisoned. Silence fell.

G. Select the correct form for each blank.

1. My _____ cars are both wrecked and in the repair shop.
   a. sister and brother's
   b. sisters' and brothers'
   c. sister's and brother's
   d. sisters and brothers

2. Every Saturday we shopped at our favorite general merchandise shop, _____ General Store in Concord.
   a. Santigo, Marco & Garena's
   b. Santigo, Marco's & Garena's
   c. Santigo's, Marco's & Garena's

3. Mary searched all over the building for the _____ room.
   a. lady's
   b. ladies
   c. ladys'
   d. ladies'

4. Every _____ budget is approved by its mayor.
   a. cities
   b. cities'
   c. city's

5. The _____ playground is in unsafe condition.
   a. children's
   b. childrens'
   c. childrens

6. Every employee is entitled to three _____ vacation.
   a. week's
   b. weeks
   c. weeks'

7. The organization for city bus _____ met last night.
   a. drivers
   b. drivers'
   c. driver's
8. The police found several fingerprints left by the _____ .
   a. thieves
   b. thiefs
   c. thief's
9. Several _____ complaints were heard by the manager.
   a. customer's
   b. customers
   c. customers'
10. Do you feel that you got your five _____ worth?
    a. dollars
    b. dollars'
    c. dollar's
11. My _____ phone number has been changed recently.
    a. sister-in-law's
    b. sister's-in-law
    c. sister's-in-law's
12. I was having lunch with _____ Black, Thomasie, and Cruz.
    a. Misters'
    b. Mister
    c. Messrs.
    d. Mr.'s

Functions of Nouns

128   We know the definition of nouns, and we know that they can be singular or plural; they can also be possessive. We now take a look at the ways in which nouns function within a sentence. Nouns are extremely versatile, and can put on many "faces" within sentences. Except for pronouns, nouns have more functions than any of the other parts of speech.

The following is a list of noun functions:

1. subject of a clause
2. direct object
3. indirect object
4. predicate nominative (also called predicate noun)
5. appositive

6. direct address
7. object of a preposition

These are the primary ways in which nouns can be used, and each will be discussed in some detail.

129   **Subject of a Clause**

When we talk about subjects, we usually mean the subject of a sentence, that is, who or what is doing the action or experiencing the "state of being." Not only sentences have subjects, however. Dependent clauses also have subjects.

SUBJECT OF A COMPLETE SENTENCE:

Mr. Jung kept us in his house for four hours listening to those tapes.
Catherine and **Maxwell** plan to be married next month.

SUBJECT OF A DEPENDENT CLAUSE:

When **Mrs. Marcos** heard about her son's accident, she flew to Denver.
I will answer that question only if **Boris** leaves the room and when **Clement** stops talking.

130   **Direct Object**

The direct object is easily found in sentences that have an active verb. Formula: Find the verb, find the subject of the verb; then say subject + verb, and ask "who" or "what."

Carmen hurled the **bowl** across the room at me.
That student never answers **questions** correctly in my class.
Marvin gave Theresa a **necklace.**

Direct objects are found not only in main clauses, but also in dependent clauses.

I heard that Paul had married **Celeste.**
Kathy Hanover announced that Elena had won the **award** for excellence.
When the door hit the **wall,** the painting fell.

Direct objects can be verbals.

I love **running.**
I love **to run.**
Martine enjoyed **reading** at night.

131   Indirect Object

The indirect object usually can be found between the verb and the direct object. Not every sentence that contains a direct object will have an indirect object, but there can never be an indirect object unless there is a direct object. The formula is: Say subject + verb + direct object, and then ask "to whom" or "to what."

> Maurice gave **Nelson** the answers to the examination.
> Did Mr. Frasier tell **Kate** the truth?

132   Predicate Nominative

The predicate nominative, sometimes called the predicate noun, renames the subject. The verb will be a "state of being" verb rather than an action verb (*am, is, are, was, were, shall be, will be, has been, was named, was elected*).

> Mrs. Korman was elected **president** of the PTA that year.
> I always thought that O'Brien kid was a **rascal**.
> My brother had been a **fireman**, an **electrician**, and a **policeman** before he became a teacher.
> The party was a **joke**; the entire party was terribly boring.
> English is my favorite **subject**; my teacher is a **clown**.

Note: Remember that the predicate nominative renames; for example, in the first example above, *Mrs. Korman* and *president* are the same person. It is easy to confuse the predicate nominative with the predicate adjective, which does not rename, but rather describes. In the fourth example, *boring* is a predicate adjective, not a predicate nominative, because it describes rather than renames.

133   Appositive

An appositive, like a predicate nominative, renames; however, it is in apposition to, or next to, the word it renames. Position, then, is the difference between an appositive and a predicate nominative. Appositives are usually, though not always, set off by commas. (See the section on commas in Unit 3, Punctuation.)

> Professor Hu, my chemistry **instructor**, did not show up for class that day.
> My brother's friend, **Samuel Davies III**, graduated with honors.
> My sister **Helen** lived with us for six years.
> Springton, a small mining **town**, is Susan's hometown.

134 Direct Address

Direct address names the person or thing being talked to in a sentence. It is followed by a comma if it occurs at the beginning of a sentence, set off with commas if in midsentence, and preceded by a comma if it occurs at the end of a sentence. Direct address can be a proper name or other term for the person or thing being spoken to.

> **Miss Corea,** please repeat the question.
> Tell me, **mister,** do you expect me to let you continue this charade?
> Will you please speak up so that we can hear you, **Tim.**
> Oh, **officer,** I didn't realize I was speeding.
> All right, **car,** don't let me down this morning!

135 Object of a Preposition

The object of a preposition completes the meaning of the preposition. The preposition and its object, and often a word or words that modify the object, constitute a prepositional phrase. (See the section on prepositions in this unit.)

> Were your glasses on the dressing **table**?
> After the **game** we went to the **cafe** downtown.
> The purse was sitting beside the **stack** of **books** near the **lamp.**

Exercise

Indicate the function of each underlined noun (SC = subject of a clause, DO = direct object, IO = indirect object, PN = predicate nominative, APP = appositive, DA = direct address, OP = object of a preposition). Place your answer above each noun.

1. We were planning a meeting for Tuesday night, but the chairman couldn't make it.

2. I couldn't seem to reach my niece on the telephone.

3. I don't think, Ms. Espino, that you understood the question.

4. Timothy O'Malley, my first cousin, was arrested for breaking and entering, but I posted bail for Timothy.

5. Kelly said that I would be elected chairman if I decided to run for that office.

6. William gave Denise a raise, but the other employees received nothing.

7. Inside the <u>book</u> were some handwritten notes, strange <u>scribblings</u>.

8. <u>To welcome</u> him warmly was my <u>job</u>.

9. I was hoping to find the money back in the <u>account</u>, but the <u>funds</u> were still missing.

10. Your <u>friend</u>, <u>Mario Inzeria</u>, was with you in the <u>car</u>, wasn't he?

11. Tell me, <u>madam</u>, did you recognize the <u>man</u> who came to your house?

12. I thought that he was a <u>policeman</u>, so I was careful about what I said.

13. Tonight we are about to discuss your difficulty with <u>Adam Ponselle</u>, the <u>man</u> on trial here in this <u>court</u>.

14. You gave your <u>mother</u> a hard time, <u>David</u>.

15. The guests sat around the <u>table</u> in those old, broken chairs.

16. The <u>desk</u> had been emptied when <u>Naomi</u> arrived at the office Wednesday.

17. <u>Pretending</u> you don't remember won't help the <u>defendant</u>.

18. <u>Dr. Cohen</u> gave <u>Mrs. Morris</u> <u>instructions</u> for the patient in Room 23.

19. You were arrested for <u>exceeding</u> the speed limit and for driving while intoxicated.

20. Lisabeth Morton and <u>Richard Uniz</u>, <u>students</u> of yours, have testified that you remained on the <u>grounds</u> until after five o'clock that night.

Pronouns

136

At first glance, pronouns might seem to be simpler to manage than other parts of speech because there are a limited number of them. Yet this is far from being the case. They are perhaps the most troublesome of all the parts of speech. Pronouns are complicated by factors such as case and pronoun-antecedent agreement. To learn to use pronouns correctly requires considerable effort, but once mastered the skill will be yours for life.

An understanding of pronouns is important to the CR for the same reason that the CR needs to know grammar in general. The CR must produce correct English as spoken by the attorneys and judges. For example, the sentence below contains a pronoun error:

No one knew who had overheard the conversation, but whomever it was knew too much.

Did you find it? The pronoun *whomever* should be *whoever*. We shall examine why later in this section.

137   The definition of pronouns is a familiar one: pronouns take the place of nouns.

> John's report lay on John's desk until John threw the report away.

Pronouns replace the noun *John* as follows:

> John's report lay on **his** desk until **he** threw the report away.

138   **Personal Pronouns**

Personal pronouns may be first-person, second-person, or third-person. First-person pronouns refer to the person(s) or being(s) *doing* the speaking. Second-person pronouns refer to the person(s) or being(s) that are being spoken *to*. Third-person pronouns refer to the person(s) or being(s) that are being spoken *about*. Table 2-7 lists the personal pronouns.

FIRST-PERSON PRONOUNS:

> **I** told Jackson about **our** plans, but he didn't believe **me**.
> **We** looked everywhere for **our** car, but **I** realized it had been stolen.

SECOND-PERSON PRONOUNS:

> **You** asked that question already in **your** interrogation yesterday.
> **You** take care of **yours**, and **you** will be just fine.

Table 2-7
Personal Pronouns

	Singular	Plural
First Person	I, my, mine, me	we, our, ours, us
Second Person	you, your, yours	you, your, yours
Third Person	he, his, him	they, their, theirs,
	she, her, hers	them
	it, its	

THIRD-PERSON PRONOUNS:

He wanted her to go with **him** to **their** cabin.

Their car was in the shop, so instead of taking **theirs**, Bill drove **his**.

She told **them** what Miss Valdez had said.

The dog ran across the street, and **it** was nearly hit by a car.

139   Case

Pronouns change in form according to their case. Case refers to the way in which a pronoun is used in a sentence—as a subject or as an object, for example. This is perhaps the most important aspect of pronouns. The issue of case is the one that the CR faces when he or she is unsure whether to use *who* or *whom*, *I* or *me*, *he* or *him*.

There are three cases: nominative, objective, and possessive (genitive).

1. **Nominative Case.** Also known as the subjective case. Pronouns in the nominative case usually function as subjects or predicate nominatives. Pronouns that can be used in the nominative case are as follows:

   FIRST PERSON: I, we

   SECOND PERSON: you

   THIRD PERSON: he, she, it, they

   INTERROGATIVE/RELATIVE PRONOUN: who, whoever

   They planned the trip carefully. (subject)
   I heard that **he** resigned, but **who** cares? (subjects)
   The only members voting against the measure were Diane, Tony, and **I**. (predicate nominative)
   The only children who were a problem in the classroom were Marcus and **she**. (predicate nominative)
   It was **I** who asked for an investigation. (predicate nominative)

2. **Objective Case.** Pronouns in the objective case are used as the direct object, indirect object, or object of a preposition. Pronouns that can be used in the objective case are as follows:

   FIRST PERSON: me, us

   SECOND PERSON: you

THIRD PERSON: him, her, it, them

INTERROGATIVE/RELATIVE PRONOUN: whom, whomever

> Jarrett told **me** the entire sordid story. (indirect object)
> Francesca believed **them**, but I had known **him** too long to be deceived. (direct objects)
> **Whom** did Loretta tell? (direct object)
> Mother sends **her** gifts every Christmas but never gets thanked for any of them. (indirect object)
> The Winstons told **us** lies about the accident, so how could I have known? (indirect object)
> Mr. Hu refused to do any favors for **us** or for **him**. (objects of prepositions)
> Juan walked around **her** and seized **her** by the shoulders. (object of preposition; direct object)
> The boys didn't want that dog near **them**. (object of preposition)

3. **Possessive (Genitive) Case.** The genitive case is the possessive form of pronouns.

   FIRST PERSON: my, mine, our, ours

   SECOND PERSON: your, yours

   THIRD PERSON: his, her, hers, its, their, theirs

   INTERROGATIVE/RELATIVE PRONOUN: whose

If a possessive pronoun is used with a noun, it acts as an adjective.

> **My** house has been remodeled recently.
> The dog broke **its** foot.
> **His** case is not as strong as **her** case, in **our** opinion.

Do not confuse possessive pronouns with contractions.

Correct

That statement was yours, not ours.

Wrong

That statement was your's, not our's.

Correct

Did you know whose coat was left on your desk?

Wrong

Did you know who's coat was left on your desk?

Correct

I understand your position, but hers is reasonable also.

Wrong

I understand you're position, but her's is reasonable also.

140   Confusion over when to use the nominative case of the pronoun and when to use the objective case is a common problem, especially with *who* and *whom*. The following sentences demonstrate common errors:

1. Who did Jim ask to assist him with the annual report?

2. The scholarship will be awarded to whomever scores highest on the examinations.

3. Vote for the person whom you think will do the best job.

4. Are you planning to make the trip with François and I?

What is wrong with the above sentences?

1. If you read the sentence in reverse order (*Jim did ask...*) you can see that the objective case of the pronoun should be used: *whom*. The corrected sentence reads:

   Whom did Jim ask to assist him with the annual report?

2. In this sentence, the word following the preposition *to* is not the object of the preposition but the subject of the verb *scores*. The nominative case of the pronoun is needed: *whoever*.

   The scholarship will be awarded to **whoever** scores highest on the examination.

3. In this sentence, the expression *you think* is parenthetical and does not affect the case of the pronoun. The pronoun functions as the subject of *will do* and should be in the nominative case: *who*.

   Vote for the person **who** you think will do the best job.

4. In this sentence, the pronoun is the object of the preposition *with* and should be in the objective case: *me*.

Are you planning to make the trip with François and **me**?

From some reason, many people are nervous about using the word *me*; they think *I* sounds more proper. An easy test is to imagine the sentence without *François and*:

Are you planning to make the trip with **me**?

There is no temptation to use *I* in that situation.

When confronted with sentences like those above, taking an extra moment to ask yourself how the pronoun functions in the sentence will clear up any confusion about correct usage.

141 Interrogative Pronouns

These are the pronouns that ask a question: *who, whose, which, what, whom.*

> **Who** is there?
> With **whom** did you speak?
> **What** did you do about the situation?
> **Which** desk did you use when you worked here?

Interrogative pronouns can function as adjectives when they are next to the noun they modify.

> **Whose** credit card was used to pay for the tickets?
> **What** car did you like best?
> **Whose** opinion counts the most in the company?

Interrogative pronouns can act as the subject of a verb.

> **Who** was at the door?
> **Which** is the better choice?

Interrogative pronouns can function as the direct object.

> **Whom** did you ask?
> **What** did the ball hit?

Interrogative pronouns can act as the object of a preposition.

> For **whom** did Ernesto do the work?
> With **what** did you hit him?

Interrogative pronouns can act as the indirect object.

> You gave **whom** the money?
> He sold **whom** the house and the land?

142 Relative Pronouns

Relative pronouns act as subordinators; that is, they cause the clauses they begin to become dependent, or subordinate, and thus unable to stand alone as complete, independent sentences. Relative pronouns include *that, whoever, whomever, who, whom,* and *which.* Note that some relative pronouns are the same as some of the interrogative pronouns. The difference is in the way they are used in the sentence.

Those boys **who** got in trouble with Mr. Ortega never forgot the incident.

Whoever the board selects will be responsible for planning the assemblies.

Jonah was the only one of my brothers **who** worked at Father's company.

Smoky was the only cat **that** stayed with us and didn't run away.

143 Demonstrative Pronouns

These serve to point: *this, that, these, those.* The demonstrative pronouns can serve as adjectives when they are placed next to a noun, but they often stand alone without a noun.

These questions have been asked already. (with noun)
These are for you. (without noun)
That dress is absolutely fabulous on you. (with noun)
That is simply untrue, Doris. (without noun)

144 Indefinite Pronouns

These pronouns refer to no specific person or thing and set no limitations. Some of the most common indefinite pronouns are:

all	either	neither	some
anybody	everybody	nobody	somebody
anyone	everyone	none	someone
both	everything	no one	something
each	many	several	

Most indefinite pronouns take a singular verb.

No one is expected to disagree with his suggestion.
Somebody is going to tell him the truth, you know.
None of the boys **is** willing to assist with the job. (*None are* is also acceptable.)
Everybody in our group **has become accustomed** to the discussion sessions.

Both, few, many, several, and *others* take a plural verb.

> **Both** my brothers **are** in college this year.
> **Few** of the students **have passed** the exam.
> **Many** of my cousins **have moved** to other parts of the country.
> **Others were leaving** before the close of the meeting.

Some indefinite pronouns can be singular or plural, depending on the content of the sentence, including the pronouns *all*, *none*, and *some*.

> **Some** of the children **were** outdoors when the ceiling collapsed.
> **Some** of the pie **is** left, and you may have it.
> **None** of your money **is** needed.

145 Reflexive and Intensive Pronouns

Reflexive and intensive pronouns are the *self* pronouns: *myself, yourself, himself, herself, ourselves, themselves, yourselves, itself.*

These pronouns are reflexive when they are used as the object of a verb and designate the same person or thing as the subject of that verb.

> When I saw that Luisa had hurt **herself**, I ran to her.
> I told **myself** that he was lying to me.
> He considered **himself** to be the best candidate for the office.

Intensive pronouns, on the other hand, are used for emphasis.

> I **myself** wrote the report.
> The governor **himself** spoke to our group.
> You told me **yourself** that he was a violent person.

146 Pronoun-Antecedent Agreement

A pronoun and its antecedent must agree in person and number.

> **I** will deliver **my** report next Thursday afternoon. (first-person singular)
> **The Jarretts** have sold **their** house in Springville. (third-person plural)

- Third-person singular pronouns must also agree in *gender* (masculine, feminine, or neuter) with the nouns they refer to. Most nouns are neuter (*rug, desk, newspaper, street*) and are replaced by a form of the neuter pronoun *it*. Some are clearly masculine (*man, waiter, actor*) or clearly feminine (*woman, waitress, actress*).

My car **engine** has thrown one of **its** rods.
Mr. Bolton lent us **his** car on several occasions.
Marianne left **her** overcoat on the bus.

Some nouns can be either masculine or feminine (*student, child, person, employee*). Whereas it was once considered "correct" to use the masculine pronoun for a noun that could be either feminine or masculine, the preferred style now is to present both alternatives.

Outdated

Each student should pick up his schedule in Allen Hall.

Current

Each student should pick up his or her schedule in Allen Hall.

● Pronoun-antecedent agreement can become a source of confusion when the antecedent is an indefinite pronoun.

1. The following take a singular pronoun: *each, either, neither, one, everyone, everybody, no one, nobody, anyone, anybody, someone, somebody.* If the gender is unclear or undetermined, use *he or she, his or her,* or *him or her.*

   No one in our troupe lost **his or her** confidence when the play closed.
   Somebody left **his or her** suitcase on the plane.
   Either Claude or Chad will drive **his** car to the airport. (clearly masculine)
   Neither Mary nor Laura likes **her** job at the factory. (clearly feminine)

2. Depending on the meaning of the sentence, use either singular or plural pronouns with the following: *none, most, all.*

   Most of the girls in my daughter's club had **their** dresses made by Ms. Coleman.
   Most of the house has had **its** exterior painted.
   All of our children are grown now and have **their** own homes.

● Collective nouns take plural pronouns unless the members of the group are clearly acting as individuals.

   The **team** is hoping to win **its** last game.
   The **team** are putting on **their** new uniforms.
   My **family** is having **its** reunion on Thanksgiving Day.
   My **family** have **their** own ideas about their careers.

Exercise

Select and underline the proper word for each sentence.

1. Do you want to go to the theatre with Jim and (I, me)?
2. It is (I, me) who needed the dictionary.
3. The chairman is (he, him).
4. Just between (we, us) members, I think that nonmembers should not be allowed to attend.
5. He did it for Eva and (I, me).
6. (We, Us) students are planning a protest tomorrow morning.
7. (Who, Whom) did you work with at Miller & Ornette?
8. I thought that jacket was (yours, your's).
9. The best candidate is (her, she).
10. (Ours, Our's) is the smallest house on the block, I think.
11. (Who, Whom) do you think will be selected?
12. The woman I saw in the back of the building was (her, she).
13. The only employees who had to stay late were Maria, Timothy, and (I, me).
14. The house was lovely, but (its, it's) price was just too high for us.
15. We received several letters from Patricia Dell and (her, she).
16. Last month our class gave (its, their) end-of-the-year program.
17. If anyone wants to leave now (he, she, they, he or she) may depart at intermission.
18. Either of my sisters could have left (her, their) coat here.
19. Catherine is in trouble, not (I, me).
20. Neither Sam nor Michael has (his, their) summer job yet.
21. Each of their children (has, have) a car.
22. Neither of my brothers (feel, feels) sure about (his, their) future in the family company.
23. Both of my brothers will have (his, their) education paid by grants.
24. The company is looking to hire three persons for (its, their) publicity department.
25. Everyone in my classes (is, are) aware of my struggle.

Verbs

147 The *verb* is one of the two main parts of a sentence, the other being the subject of the verb. Without a verb, a group of words cannot be a complete sentence. The *complete verb* includes all the words in a sentence that, combined, tell what was done or describe a condition or state of being. The *complete subject* includes all the words that, combined, tell about whom or what the sentence is speaking. Thus, simple sentences can be divided into two distinct parts—complete subject and complete verb. (For purposes of this book, the term *predicate* will not be discussed or distinguished from the term *verb*.)

Mr. Unoji and his wife / have opened a grocery store.
(complete subject)   (complete verb)

The simple subject and simple verb are the main or primary word(s) in the complete subject and verb, without modifiers or phrases or parentheticals. For example, in the example above, the simple subject and simple verb are:

Mr. Unoji, wife / have opened

Henceforth in this text the term *verb* will refer to the simple verb, and the term *subject* will refer to the simple subject.

148 **Inverted Order**

Usually the verb follows the subject, but inverted sentences reverse this order.

Several motorcycle owners live on my block.

INVERTED: On my block live several motorcycle owners.

Inversion does not change the form of the verb or the meaning of the sentence. When dealing with an inverted sentence, if confusion occurs about the form of the verb that should be employed, turn the sentence around in your head to normal order. Whatever verb seems correct in normal order will be correct in the inverted form as well.

149 **Auxiliary Verbs**

Auxiliary verbs, or helping verbs, are used along with other verbs to help in forming the various tenses, moods, etc. A list of the 23 common auxiliary verbs can be found in the Glossary. An auxiliary verb is part of the simple verb, and a main verb can have more than one auxiliary verb.

Oscar Burgos **was** helping with the boys' baseball team.
Sally White **can** tell you what happened.

You **must** consider what we **are** proposing.

It **could have been** managed with more skill.

We **must have** had a problem with the wiring in the radio.

Some of the verbs used as auxiliaries are verbs in their own right and are often used alone, not as "helpers."

She **is** president of her sorority this year.

He **was** a capable organizer, but not well liked.

150 **Subject-Verb Agreement**

Subjects and verbs within a sentence must agree in person and in number. In other words, a singular subject takes a singular verb, and a plural subject takes a plural verb. This sounds simple—and it generally is.

The young **boy was** playing baseball in the field. (singular subject and verb)

The young **boys were** playing baseball in the field. (plural subject and verb)

A compound subject takes a plural verb.

My **brother** and **William Tabir were going** to the game room.

Buffalo and **Albany were added** to the tour.

● Sentences that begin with "There" often cause confusion. To remedy this situation, the CR should consider the sentence as it would read "turned around."

There is a problem with those pieces of correspondence.

THINK: A problem is there with the pieces of correspondence.

There were no greater confusions in my mind than what he intended.

THINK: No greater confusions were there in my mind than what he intended.

● Another source of confusion in subject-verb agreement is in the use of collective nouns. Most collective nouns take a singular verb, but a few take plural verbs. The test is to decide whether the members act as a group or as individuals. The distinction is not always perfectly clear, but the CR should give the matter some thought and try to come to a conclusion; if no clear conclusion can be made, use the singular verb. (See the section on collective nouns in this unit.)

The **orchestra were putting** on their uniforms.
The entire **staff are working** on their job descriptions.
The **committee is meeting** tonight to elect officers.

- Subject-verb agreement can be clouded by correlatives. If both subjects are singular, then use a singular verb. (See the section on conjunctions in this unit.)

  Either Jane **or** Kate **is** going to be elected.
  Neither the station wagon **nor** the sedan **was** in shape
  for such an extended journey.

- If both subjects are plural, use a plural verb.

  Neither my **students** nor my **children were** aware of
  my health problems.
  Either the **Harrisons** or the **Tates were** planning to
  host the meeting.

- If one of the subjects is singular and the other one is plural, the verb should agree with the one that is *closer* to the verb in the sentence.

  Neither the **agent** nor the **clients have** an understanding of the contract.
  Neither the **clients** nor the **agent has** an understanding of the contract.
  Either the **bookkeeper** or the **accountants do** the job.
  Either the **accountants** or the **bookkeeper does** the job.

- Considerable confusion in subject-verb agreement is caused by intervening words—that is, words that occur between the subject and verb. These are usually phrases. If intervening words cause a problem, just imagine the sentence without those words. Find the subject and the verb of the main clause, ignoring for the moment the elements that fall between, and check to see if the subject and verb agree.

  The **book** of photographs of my family—including my
  grandparents and dozens of cousins—**was sitting**
  on the coffee table when I last saw it.

In the example above, the subject is *book*, so the verb must be singular: *was sitting*.

  That rickety old **shelf** holding up the hundreds of books
  that we inherited **is** just about to fall down.
  A parking **lot** full of cars **was** the scene of the robbery.

Mario's **friends**, including Peter, **become** rowdy when they drink.

Mr. **Johnson**, accompanied by his bodyguards, **was trying** to enter the church after the wedding was in progress.

- Compound subjects that speak of a *single* person or entity, and not of plural persons or things, should be considered a singular subject and thus take a singular verb.

    The group's founder and current president **is** Olivia Marshall.

    Note: In the example above, the founder and president is the same individual—Olivia Marshall. If two different individuals were the subject, the verb would be plural.

    The group's founder and current president **are** Olivia Marshall and Teri Langlois, respectively.

    Ham and eggs **is** my favorite breakfast.

    My friend and confidante, Sylvia Jean, **has brought** me through many catastrophes.

- Titles of books, movies, songs, magazines, newspapers, or other similar titles may be plural in form, but they take a singular verb because they represent a single entity.

    "Children of the Corn" **was** a frightening movie.

    "The Northwest Counties" **is distributed** weekly at local stores.

    "The Big Cats" **was** an excellent television program and of interest to animal lovers of any age.

    Note: Titles are traditionally underlined or italicized in print, but CRs use quotation marks. (See the section on quotation marks in Unit 3, Punctuation.)

- Relative pronouns often are used as the subject of a dependent clause. Deciding what verb is correct is sometimes not easy. Use the verb that would be appropriate to the antecedent of the relative pronoun.

    The man who **is sitting** next to Mr. Veriana accosted my brother.

In the example above, the antecedent of *who* is *man*; thus, the verb should be singular.

    I, who **am** an only child, have always envied people from large families.

In the example above, the antecedent of *who* is *I*; thus, the first-person singular verb is used.

Subject-verb agreement can be tricky after the expression *one of*.

Correct

He is one of those people who always **have** something to complain about. (The relative pronoun *who* refers to *people*, not to *one*, so the plural verb *have* is used.)

Wrong

He is one of those people who always has something to complain about.

BUT:

Gil behaves as though he is the only man in the United States who **is going** through a divorce.

She is the only one of my friends who never **forgets** my birthday.

- Indefinite pronouns usually take singular verbs, although a few of them take plural verbs. (See the section on pronouns in this unit.)

Everybody on the tour **was** responsible for his or her own luggage.

Each of the dogs **is going** to be vaccinated by the vet this week.

- A predicate nominative that does not agree in number with its subject can cause confusion. The verb should agree in number with the subject, *not* with the predicate nominative.

His biggest **complaint was** the mosquitos in the area.

The **mosquitos** in the area **were** his biggest complaint.

The biggest **danger** to entry **was** the attack dogs.

The attack **dogs were** the biggest danger.

- Sometimes plural subjects are used to mean a single unit. In such cases, use a singular verb.

Ten cents is the price of the gum.

Ten pennies are sitting on the table.

Two hours is the time needed for the interview.

Two hours are not likely to pass quickly.

- Fractions are handled by looking at the word to which they refer.

One fourth of my **salary** goes into my savings account. (singular)

One fourth of the **students** are failing. (plural)

151   Tense

Tense refers to time. Every verb has three principal parts: the present tense, past tense, and past participle. The past participle is used with an auxiliary (helping) verb.

Regular verbs usually form the past tense and past participle by adding *ed* to the present form:

Present	Past	Past Participle
work	worked	worked
help	helped	helped
open	opened	opened
wish	wished	wished
clean	cleaned	cleaned

This list could go on and on, but there would be little point in that. In sentences, they are used as follows:

I **work** every day from eight to five. (present)

I **worked** the night shift for several years. (past)

I have **worked** there ever since I finished school. (past participle with auxiliary verb)

The problem with tense occurs with verbs whose forms do not follow this regular pattern. There are more than two hundred such verbs in English. Table 2-8 gives a sampling of irregular verbs. The dictionary lists the forms with the present-tense entry of a verb. For example, if you look up *eat*, the dictionary entry will give *ate* and *eaten*, the past and past participle forms of that verb. Doubt about troublesome verbs can be resolved by checking the dictionary.

The six tenses are: present, past, future, present perfect, past perfect, and future perfect. There is no need for the CR to spend a lot of time on tenses, but listed below are examples of each tense:

PRESENT: Nora **paints** portraits now, not landscapes.

PAST: Nora **painted** landscapes in art school.

FUTURE: Nora **will paint** a portrait of my daughter.

PRESENT PERFECT: She **has painted** several portraits this winter.

PAST PERFECT: She **had painted** landscapes for several years before she turned to portraits.

FUTURE PERFECT: When Nora completes the portrait of my daughter, she **will have painted** 50 portraits.

Table 2-8
Irregular Verbs

Present	Past	Past Participle
am	was	been
are	were	been
become	became	become
begin	began	begun
break	broke	broken
bring	brought	brought
burst	burst	burst
buy	bought	bought
choose	chose	chosen
come	came	come
do	did	done
draw	drew	drawn
drink	drank	drunk
drive	drove	driven
eat	ate	eaten
fall	fell	fallen
freeze	froze	frozen
give	gave	given
go	went	gone
grow	grew	grown
know	knew	known
lay	laid	laid
leave	left	left
lie	lay	lain
make	made	made
pay	paid	paid
ride	rode	ridden
ring	rang	rung
run	ran	run
see	saw	seen
send	sent	sent
set	set	set
shine	shone	shone
sing	sang	sung
speak	spoke	spoken
spring	sprang	sprung
steal	stole	stolen
swim	swam	swum
take	took	taken
wear	wore	worn
write	wrote	written

152   Voice

Verbs can be active or passive. A subject with an active verb is performing the action. A subject with a passive verb is having the action done to him, her, or it.

ACTIVE: Juan mowed five lawns today.

PASSIVE: Our lawn was mowed by Juan.

ACTIVE: The typewriter fell from the desk.

PASSIVE: The typewriter was dropped by Paula.

Exercises

A. Select and underline the correct verb for each sentence.

1. There (is, are) a lot of boys in our yard.

2. There (is, are) a lot of soup in the pot.

3. There (is, are) a dollar bill in your wallet.

4. There (is, are) five one-dollar bills in your wallet.

5. My brother, and the pest that drives me crazy, (is, are) named Jason.

6. The team (is, are) putting on their shoes.

7. Each boy and girl (is, are) going to be questioned individually.

8. A pair of scissors (is, are) sitting in your sewing basket.

9. Alan's toys, including his basketball, (is, are) scattered throughout the kitchen.

10. Economics (is, are) my worst course.

11. The left tire, not to mention the brakes and shocks, (has, have) to be replaced.

12. Neither the president nor the members (has, have) any ideas about how to raise money for the club.

13. Television, even Saturday cartoons, (becomes, become) tiresome after a couple of hours.

14. The owner of that house and a millionaire in his own right (is, are) my cousin Winston Perron.

15. Either the watch or the bracelets (is, are) going to have to be removed.

16. Many children, including my son, (does, do) poor work if the radio is on.

17. Mary is one of those workers who (has, have) a genuinely positive attitude toward the job.

18. You, who (knows, know) the truth, cannot remain silent.

19. That's only one of the five books which (is, are) to be read for the novels course this semester.

20. A shelf stacked with encyclopedia volumes (is, are) about to fall.

21. "The Williams Boys" (is, are) a new TV program.

22. My problem (is, are) those bugs.

23. That bunch of roses (has, have) fallen onto the floor.

24. The men who are running for chairman (is, are) speaking tonight.

25. "Just One of the Girls" (has, have) run a long time.

26. Twenty-four hours (is, are) not enough time for me to get the money.

27. Six hours (has, have) passed since we called Mr. Forbes.

28. Two thirds of the teachers (has, have) been denied a raise.

29. I, who (is, am) usually proficient, failed miserably.

30. He was the only one of our clients who (was, were) prompt with payments.

B. The present tense of the verb is listed to the left of each sentence. Fill in the blank with the correct form of that verb.

lie
1. He has _____ on the bed staring at the ceiling for most of the day.

burst
2. She has _____ my bubble with her lack of enthusiasm.

begin
3. I had _____ to like the job until my supervisor resigned.

lay
4. That old newspaper has _____ on the dining room table since Sunday.

break
5. You will have _____ every rule in the book if you do that.

pay
6. Ellen has _____ for everything, and she cannot afford it.

steal	7. Andy has _____ all of my ideas!
swim	8. I had never _____ that far or long before.
drive	9. After we have _____ around the block a couple of times, can we take the car out on the highway?
go	10. David has _____ to all of his concerts.
wear	11. I've _____ this dress to every formal function at the university for the past five years.
ride	12. The horses were _____ too hard by those boys, so refuse to rent to them.
choose	13. Rodriguez has been _____ to lead the neighborhood meeting.
shine	14. The sun _____ brightly every morning last week, but there were showers every afternoon.
slay	15. The criminal admits to having _____ the three students.
set	16. I _____ my purse down and now it's gone.
rise	17. The water _____ three feet during the night.
leave	18. Candy had _____ her pets with me for three weeks.
raise	19. Nell's salary was _____ by 8 percent.
is	20. Carl has _____ married three times.

Adjectives

153   Adjectives serve to modify, describe, limit, or define nouns and pronouns. They and adverbs behave as modifiers. There are five basic classifications of adjectives: descriptive, proper, articles, possessive, and demonstrative.

154   **Descriptive Adjectives**

Most adjectives are descriptive: *blue, pretty, bright, brief, soft, expensive, small, gigantic, silly, favorite, well-qualified, oily, rocky, old, young, wet, tough, insane, brief.* There are hundreds more. Nouns can be transformed into adjectives:

> The **velvet** is too heavy. (noun)
> The **velvet** chair is faded and torn. (adjective)

The **color** of the walls is shocking. (noun)
The **colorful** painting clashes with the rest of the room.
  (adjective)
The **cat** endures no confinement whatsoever. (noun)
Her **catlike** movements were graceful and smooth.
  (adjective)

Even verbs can be transformed into adjectives.

I **walk** to school, even in the snow. (verb)
His **walking** stick is a beautiful, carved creation. (adjective)
We were **running** five miles a day then. (verb)
My **running** shoes are ruined! (adjective)

- Descriptive adjectives come in three forms, or degrees: positive, comparative, and superlative. See Table 2-9 for examples. The comparative form compares two people or objects; the superlative is preferred when examining three or more. To form the comparative, the suffix *er* is added to words with one or two syllables. There are exceptions, notably two-syllable words that end with *ful* or *less* (*careful, faithful, hapless, loveless*). The comparative form of these words is formed by adding *more*. For words of more than two syllables, the word *more* is combined with the positive form of the adjective. Other words seem to follow no rule (*little, less, least; bad, worse, worst*).

   The superlative form of adjectives, which examines three or more persons or things, often is formed by adding the *est* suffix to the positive form. For words of more than two syllables, employ the word *most* with the positive form. The same exceptions apply as for the comparative.

   John is the **youngest** of the five brothers.
   John is the **younger** of the two men.
   Which automobile is **smaller**—yours or mine?
   Which automobile is **smallest**—yours, mine, or Harry's?
   Ann is a **careful** driver, but Karen is **more careful**.
   I think I'm the **most careful** of all of us.

   Some adjectives cannot have a superlative or comparative form, adjectives such as *perfect, unique, dead, invisible, single, infinite,* and *universal*. These are "absolutes" and thus cannot be compared. Something cannot be more perfect than something else or more dead.

- Although adjectives usually precede the word they modify, they sometimes follow it.

   The dog, growling and furious, stood before us.
   Their house, dark and ominous, was far from inviting.

Table 2-9
Degrees of Adjectives

Positive	Comparative	Superlative
bad	worse	worst
belligerent	more belligerent	most belligerent
bold	bolder	boldest
busy	busier	busiest
careless	more careless	most careless
difficult	more difficult	most difficult
excited	more excited	most excited
faithful	more faithful	most faithful
fine	finer	finest
good	better	best
hot	hotter	hottest
intelligent	more intelligent	most intelligent
large	larger	largest
late	later	latest
little	less	least
lovely	lovelier	loveliest
much	more	most
nice	nicer	nicest
old	older	oldest
painful	more painful	most painful
pleasant	more pleasant	most pleasant
quick	quicker	quickest
selfish	more selfish	most selfish
slim	slimmer	slimmest
small	smaller	smallest
strong	stronger	strongest

The supervisor, red-faced and stammering, confronted Roy.

- If several adjectives precede a noun, they are separated by commas in most cases. However, if an adjective modifies both a noun and an adjective, no comma is employed. (See the section on commas in Unit 3, Punctuation.)

    I live in the large yellow house on the corner. (*large* modifies *yellow house*, not just *house*)
    The dark, threatening, cloud-filled sky forbade us to go on our drive.

That pouting, sullen child belongs to my sister, Donna.
Eleanor purchased an expensive fur coat last month, but
her economical, hard-working husband returned the
coat.

155 Proper Adjectives

Because proper adjectives are formed from proper nouns, most are
uppercased. There are some exceptions, such as *biblical* (from *Bible*) and
congressional (from *Congress*). Some proper adjectives have become so
commonly used that they are lowercased—*china* plates, *oriental* rugs.

She was dating a **Virginian** farmer whose name I cannot
recall right now.
Grandpa enjoyed having a **Cuban** cigar now and then,
but they were hard to find.
Did the man speak with a **German** accent?

156 Articles

There are only three adjectives that are articles: *the, a, an*. The definite article is *the*, the indefinite articles are *a* and *an*.

Mack selected **the** crew for **the** job. (a definite crew, a definite, specific job)
A playground will be built on **an** available patch of land.
(The playground and patch of land are both nonspecific,
or indefinite.)

157 Possessive Adjectives

These are the forms of pronouns that show possession when attached
to a noun.

My parents did not associate with **his** family.
Their proposal was not **her** idea of a proper solution.

158 Demonstrative Adjectives

Demonstrative pronouns used before the noun they modify act as
adjectives.

These houses were built by **those** men.
This dog knocked over **that** garbage can.

159   Predicate Adjectives

When adjectives do not precede a noun, but rather complete the verb, they are called predicate adjectives. Often confused with the predicate nominative, which renames the subject, the predicate adjective describes the subject.

You look utterly confused.

COMPARE:

> You are **lovely**. (predicate adjective)
> You are our **chairman**. (predicate nominative)

PREDICATE ADJECTIVES:

> The coincidence was **weird** and we were **shocked**.
> The dinner tasted **terrific**, and everyone seemed **relaxed**.
> The climate is **warmer** here in Tennessee than in Pennsylvania.
> Mrs. Yeager became **ruthless** and **aggressive**; once she was **kind** and **generous**.

160   Numbers

Numbers can act as adjectives.

> We planted **three** trees in our yard that day.
> Our **two** children hid behind the automobile.

Note the difference between the two sentences below. In the first, *three* acts as an adjective; in the second, *three* acts as a noun—the subject of the sentence.

> Three plans were discussed.
> Three were discussed.

161   Compound Adjectives

Compound adjectives usually are hyphenated when they precede the noun they modify, except when the first element ends with *ly*. Predicate adjectives usually are not hyphenated. Words beginning with *self-* are always hyphenated.

> Sara was running a **low-grade** fever. (precedes noun)
> We offer **up-to-date** information. (precedes noun)
> Our information is always **up to date**. (predicate adjective)
> I teach a small class of **highly motivated** students. (*ly* ending)
> He's a **self-confident** person and seems **self-assured** to me. (*self-* words)

162 Adjectives After Linking Verbs

Linking verbs are verbs of being and verbs that pertain to the senses: *be, become, seem, remain, look, appear, smell, feel, taste, sound.* It is important to remember that linking verbs are followed by adjectives (predicate adjectives), not adverbs.

Correct

I feel **bad** about the way we treated him.

Wrong

I feel badly about the way we treated him.

More Rules About Adjectives

163 Don't confuse adjectives and adverbs.

> He plays tennis **well**. (adverb)
> The pie tastes **good**. (adjective)
> I feel **bad**. (adjective)
> He sang **badly** today. (adverb)

164 When two compound adjectives with the same second element modify the same word, the second element may be used only once, but the hyphen is used twice. The first hyphen in the following sentences is called a suspension hyphen.

> At the meeting we discussed both **short-** and **long-term** goals.
> She was willing to accept either a **part-** or **full-time** job.

165 Compound adjectives can sometimes comprise several words.

> She had a **not-so-sure-of-herself** look on her face.
> I had that **gotta-get-out-of-here** feeling that night at the party.

166 Do not use *a* or *an* after *of* in the expressions *kind of* or *sort of.*

Correct

What kind of person do you think I am?

Wrong

What kind of a person do you think I am?

Correct

What sort of meal do you prefer?

Wrong

What sort of a meal do you prefer?

167   The words *first* and *last* are sometimes used with numerical adjectives. They should always be written before, not after, the numerical adjective.

Correct

Please study the first ten pages of the book.

Wrong

Please study the ten first pages in the book.

Correct

We were the last two people to be accepted.

Wrong

We were the two last people to be accepted.

168   Do not confuse possessive adjectives with contractions.

> **Who's** being invited to the reception? (contraction)
> **Whose** suggestion was this? (possessive adjective)
> **You're** the type of person we were seeking to hire. (contraction)
> **Your** proposal will be studied by the committee. (possessive adjective)
> **It's** been an excellent year for the company. (contraction)
> The association will have **its** annual convention in September. (possessive adjective)

Exercises

A. Select and underline the correct word for each of the following sentences.

1. Do you think that Martha's or Yuri's report is (best, better)?

2. Of these three shirts, which do you think is the (nicest, nicer)?

3. I was hoping to be (more slim, slimmer) by the beginning of summer.

4. Those (kind, kinds) of dogs are notorious for their fierce dispositions.

5. He grows (bolder, more bold) with each successful venture.

6. I found the atmosphere there (pleasanter, more pleasant) than in our previous corporate headquarters.

7. We own two cars, but the red one is the (worst, worse) when it comes to reliability.

8. She used some kind of conditioning lotion on her hair to make it look (more silky, silkier, silkiest).

9. That (kind of, kind of a) report should not be published, in my opinion.

10. Which of your three brothers is (older, oldest)?

11. (Who's, Whose) telephone number were you dialing when Warren walked into the room?

12. Didn't you tear out the (last five, five last) pages of Joanna's diary and burn them?

13. We both know that (its, it's) just a matter of time before his deception is uncovered.

14. Those (types of, type of) books are too difficult for a child of his age.

15. I resent getting stuck with this (hard to start, hard-to-start) automobile, especially as the weather becomes (more cold, colder).

B. Identify the predicate adjectives and predicate nominatives in the following sentences by writing PA or PN above the word.

1. Uncle Joe looked tired and worried after he talked to his son.

2. The infant was sleeping quietly.

3. The fur felt soft, warm, and expensive!

4. Langston was elected chairman of the committee, but she did not accept the office.

5. You are a scoundrel and a liar, and I refuse to believe you.

6. The trip to San Francisco was hectic, but it was enjoyable.

7. Cigarette smoking is my worst habit.

8. Rae's dog is a little monster, but she loves it.

9. The sky is growing darker and more threatening with each hour.

10. Bailey's replies were unfathomable mutterings.

11. The new rules for the office are strict and unhealthy for our morale.

12. Pepe is the best trainer in our group.

13. Maddie is friendly, but reserved at the same time.

14. I became too excited to notice that the boy was injured.

15. The song was a haunting melody that entranced all of us.

16. My husband is an excellent tennis player, but I'm a champion.

17. The new partner in the firm is Miss Armen, a young woman whose career is a brilliant example.

18. I don't know if I am capable of this assignment.

19. One student group was courteous, but the other group was overly boisterous, so they were asked to leave.

20. The apartment was vacant, but it was a wreck nonetheless.

C. Find and underline all the adjectives in the passage below.

We parked our new car in the lot, where a bright light shone down on it. The children, exhausted and dozing, were anxious to get to the clean beds inside. The ancient night watchman smiled faintly at us as we dragged into the orange-colored hallway. Our haggard faces told the story. We were weary. As he pulled back the crisp sheets, a worried expression crossed Bill's face. He wondered if the car was safe. I walked over to the tinted window and peered into the dark night, but I couldn't see the car. We decided that we were being silly and somewhat fanatical. The needed sleep made us eager to get outside the next morning. I felt excited and anxious to get out into the warm, clear morning sunshine. Then I saw my shiny new car with its side windows broken and smashed. A pitiful groan somehow came out of my gasping mouth. Villainous, hateful, monstrous thieves!

Adverbs

169   Adverbs, like adjectives, are modifiers. The difference between the two lies in what they modify. Whereas adjectives modify nouns and pronouns, adverbs modify verbs, adjectives, or other adverbs. Confusion between adjectives and adverbs often leads to errors. When an adverb modifies a verb, it usually answers one of these questions: how, when, where, or to what degree.

They performed **poorly** that night, so the crowd
responded **indifferently**. (how)
We will meet in the conference room **today.** (when)
Why don't you sit **here**? (where)
I can **barely** hear you. (to what degree)

● When an adverb modifies an adjective, it limits the adjective.

Terribly hot days make me feel ill.
He's a **truly** honest man and I admire him.

● Adverbs also modify other adverbs.

She spoke **very** calmly.
I **almost** always see him in the station.

170   **Forming Adverbs**

Adverbs usually can be formed from descriptive adjectives by adding
the suffix *ly* to the adjective form.

Miss Ewan became a **bitter** spinster. (adjective)
She laughed **bitterly** at his words. (adverb)
I always thought of Tom as a **loud** boor. (adjective)
He shouted **loudly** but no one heard him. (adverb)

MORE EXAMPLES:

Adjective	Adverb
strict parent	adhering strictly
separate rooms	going separately to the party
graceful dancer	dancing gracefully
busy office	working busily
silent hallway	walking silently

171   The adverb *not* is sometimes mistakenly thought of as part of the verb.
Its actual function is to modify the verb.

We have **not** heard from Elsa in about two weeks.
Cindy should **not** have said those things to Kirk.

172   Adverbs, like adjectives, can be compared. The degrees of adverbs are
the same as those of adjectives: positive, comparative, and superlative.

POSITIVE: We will work **quietly** in my office.

COMPARATIVE: We will work **more quietly** today than we
did last night.

SUPERLATIVE: Sheila can work the **most quietly** of the four
of us.

Remember that the comparative form involves two persons or things; the superlative involves three or more persons or things. Usually the comparative is formed by using the word *more* and the superlative by using the word *most*. There are a few adverbs, however, that form the comparative with *er* and the superlative with *est* (*soon, late, fast, low, far*).

173   Not all adverbs end with *ly*; for example, *close, deep, straight, well, almost, soon, far, late, again, down, near, now, seldom, then, up, ever, never, often, so, there, always, here, not, rather, too.*

> Go **left** at Barrow Street.
> I will explain that to you **soon**.
> Debbie was **often** late for appointments.

Exercises

A. Form adverbs from the following adjectives.

1. timid	9. probable
2. positive	10. poor
3. brief	11. hard
4. gloomy	12. cheap
5. dull	13. fast
6. foolish	14. warm
7. neat	15. strange
8. false	

B. Underline all the adverbs in the following passage and indicate whether each modifies a verb, an adjective, or another adverb by writing V, ADJ, or ADV above the word.

I walked quietly into the house. I was then afraid that Bradley might return soon, so I worked fast. I really feared him. I should have gotten my things sooner, but I was so confused. I still could hardly believe the terrible things that had happened. I was very tired and awfully worried. Suddenly the phone was ringing loudly. I didn't know whether to answer it or not. Only my youngest sister, Claire, knew where I was. Maybe she was calling. I stumbled frantically toward the telephone, but just stood there staring vacantly at the loudly ringing machine. Was it Claire? Maybe it was Bradley. Probably it was neither of them. I was genuinely bewildered. The ringing stopped. I uneasily turned toward the very familiar staircase. I wanted to take my clothes and personal possessions, a moderate request, I think.

C. Select and underline the right word for each sentence.

1. He does (good, well) in school, but he does (poor, poorly) in athletics.

2. I (sure, surely) hope that you know what you are doing.

3. I felt (bad, badly) about embarrassing Melissa in front of Torrence and Elaine.

4. We are (real, really) excited about the upcoming wedding in our family.

5. Mallory is known for her musical ability, but tonight she played (bad, badly).

6. The haircut and new dress give Nan a (complete, completely) new look.

7. Stand (close, closely) to me when he enters the room.

8. We knew that we would have to work (steadier, more steadily) if we hoped to complete it on time.

9. That child's plight is the (more, most) pitiful of all the children we have tried to help here.

10. I think that we can purchase some jewelry (cheap, cheaply) if we buy it from this dealer.

11. I found working with Carmen (pleasanter, more pleasant) than with any of the other assistants I've had.

12. How (quick, quickly) can my car be repaired?

13. Mary was suffering from headaches, and she felt (awful, awfully) that night.

14. You shouldn't feel (bad, badly) about getting the promotion that Debra hoped to have.

15. Little Deanie looked (sweet, sweetly) in her costume.

D. Decide whether each underlined word is an adverb (ADV) or an adjective (ADJ).

1. Marianne doesn't work <u>well</u> under pressure, but she is a <u>good</u> worker <u>otherwise</u>.

2. He is <u>almost</u> <u>ready</u> for your <u>best</u> ideas to be presented <u>tonight</u>.

3. It seems <u>good</u> that you have come <u>so</u> <u>soon</u>.

4. The tension was <u>unbearably</u> <u>heavy</u> when Kyle entered the room.

5. I felt <u>so</u> <u>good</u> that morning that I could <u>hardly</u> sit <u>still</u>.

6. It was <u>so</u> <u>nice</u> of you to come to my <u>humble</u> home this <u>lovely</u> morning.

7. I understand you <u>perfectly</u> and <u>fully</u>, but you seem <u>odd</u> to my friends.

8. The party was <u>so</u> <u>poorly</u> planned that no one enjoyed it.

9. The music sounded <u>sweet</u> but <u>eerie</u>.

10. He mumbled <u>angrily</u> about Rita's <u>abrupt</u> decision <u>yesterday</u>.

11. I cannot swim <u>well</u> <u>now</u>, but I was <u>formerly</u> a <u>real</u> champion.

12. I was <u>only</u> <u>partially</u> relieved at the news.

13. Most children enjoy playing <u>outdoors</u>, but Karrie <u>almost</u> <u>always</u> preferred to play in her room.

14. The <u>brightest</u> hope in my <u>entire</u> life was that scholarship.

15. We were <u>truly</u> <u>sorry</u> to hear of your <u>recent</u> loss.

Prepositions

174 Prepositions are rather difficult to define. They combine with other words to form prepositional phrases. A preposition shows the relation of a noun or pronoun (the object of the preposition) to another part of the sentence. Prepositional phrases always begin with a preposition and are completed by a noun, pronoun, or noun equivalent—the object of the preposition, which can be either singular or compound. Prepositions can consist of more than one word. Table 2-10 is a list of common one-word prepositions. Table 2-11 lists common prepositions consisting of more than one word.

> We heard about Julia's accident **from** Ms. Cruz.
> **Across** the street is a grocery, but Fred refuses to enter it because he dislikes the owner.
> Have you received any correspondence **from** Pamela or him?
> **Between** you and me, I didn't expect Miguel to show up.

Table 2-10
Common One-Word Prepositions

about	by	past
above	concerning	round
across	down	since
after	during	through
against	except	throughout
along	for	till
among	from	to
around	in	toward
at	inside	towards
before	into	under
behind	like	underneath
below	near	until
beneath	of	up
beside	off	upon
besides	on	with
between	out	without
beyond	outside	
but	over	

Table 2-11
Multi-Word Prepositions

along with	but for	in spite of
apart from	by way of	instead of
as for	in place of	on account of
as to	in reference to	to the extent that
as well as	in regard to	with regard to

Prepositional phrases can act as adjective phrases, adverbial phrases, etc. This text will not go into an analysis of those functions because that would be of little value to the CR.

175   One of the most confusing aspects of prepositions is that the same words that act as prepositions can act as other parts of speech.

He left his bicycle **outside** the garage. (preposition)
Leave your bicycle **outside**. (adverb)
But for this five-dollar bill, I am broke. (part of two-word preposition *but for*)

I am nearly broke, **but** I do have this five-dollar bill.
(conjunction)
To run a five-minute mile was his goal. (part of infinitive)
He asked me **to** the dance, but I had other plans.
(preposition)

176   **Object of a Preposition**

The noun or pronoun that completes the prepositional phrase is the object of the preposition. It is seldom difficult to locate the object of the preposition once the prepositional phrase has been found. If the object of the preposition is a pronoun, it must be in the objective case. (See the section on pronouns in this unit.)

Go along with **them** to the **movies**, Dara.
Between **you** and **me**, I didn't expect Miguel to show up.
Have you received any correspondence from **Pamela** since
she departed?

General Rules for Prepositions

177   Some people consider it poor form to end a sentence with a preposition, especially in formal writing. Most modern authorities, however, consider this practice entirely acceptable, pointing out that a sentence with a preposition at the end is often far more effective and less "stilted" than a sentence with a buried preposition. The CR should follow the preference of the speaker.

Formal

To whom did you speak?

Informal

Whom did you speak to?

Formal

For what committee did you work?

Informal

What committee did you work for?

178   *Different from* is correct when comparing, not *different than.*

Correct

Your position is no different from mine.

Wrong

Your position is no different than mine.

Correct

Although the twins are identical otherwise, Jan's haircut is different from Amy's.

Wrong

Although the twins are identical otherwise, Jan's haircut is different than Amy's.

179   Avoid using unnecessary prepositions such as *at* and *of*.

Correct

Where is Hector right now?

Wrong

Where is Hector at right now?

Correct

His name was taken off the list of candidates.

Wrong

His name was taken off of the list of candidates.

Correct

Where has he gone tonight?

Wrong

Where has he gone to tonight?

180   Do not use *of* in place of *have* after *might, could, should,* or *must.*

Correct

He could have come to the reception for Professor Dodd.

Wrong

He could of come to the reception for Professor Dodd.

Correct

I might have expected something like that to occur.

Wrong

I might of expected something like that to occur.

181 Do not confuse the prepositions *between* and *among*. Use *between* for situations in which two share; use *among* for situations in which three or more share.

> The money was divided **between** Ada and Matilde.
> There was great disagreement **among** David and his four brothers.

182 Do not use *in* and *into* interchangeably. *Into* indicates movement from one location to another; *in* means inside or within.

> We rushed **into** the house to find Gloria.
> She was **in** the dining room putting jewelry **into** the box.

183 Use *plan to*, not *plan on*.

Correct

> We were planning to drive to Arizona at the end of the week.

Wrong

> We were planning on driving to Arizona at the end of the week.

184 Use *independent of*, not *independent from*.

Correct

> He planned to start his own firm, one that would be independent of his father's company.

Wrong

> He planned to start his own firm, one that would be independent from his father's company.

185 *Correspond with* means to write letters back and forth; *correspond to* means to match with something.

> What we have received does not correspond **to** what we ordered.
> I have corresponded **with** Paul Yoman for nine years.

186 Use *accompanied with* to indicate being with an object; use *accompanied by* to indicate being with a person.

> The machine was accompanied **with** a user's manual.
> Pillot will be accompanied **by** Mr. Hu and Miss Sorrell.

187 Write *angry with* a person, *angry at* a situation.

He's been angry **with** his sister for a month now.
The chairman became angry **at** the noise downstairs.

Exercises

A. In the following passage, find the prepositional phrases. For each phrase, underline the preposition once and its object twice.

Everything was quiet in the house, or so it seemed. We stood on the porch debating whether we should knock on the door. Dori peered through the window, trying to see if Mel was there, but everything was dark. We walked around the house. If anyone was inside the kitchen, we would probably hear them. We were looking for any indication that someone was there. Near the garage was Mel's bicycle, and beside it was another bike. I wondered who had been with him. I looked at Dori and asked her if she thought we should just knock on the door. She was torn between running and knocking. I wanted to get away from that house. In my opinion, Mel was not someone I wanted to see. I suggested that we walk to the corner and use the pay phone to call Mel. If he was at home, he'd answer. If not, we could go. Suddenly across the yard we saw a movement. Someone was among the trees at the edge of Mel's yard. I pushed past Dori to run toward the street. Behind me Dori ran, too.

B. Select and underline the proper pronoun to serve as the object of the preposition in each of the following sentences.

1. He refused to go out with Janet and (I, me).

2. Between Allegra and (she, her), they haven't a dollar.

3. He refuses to do any favors for Rick and (I, me).

4. The ball was thrown close to Neil and (she, her).

5. No one except Adam and (I, me) spoke in defense of Miss Quana.

6. Sometimes I believe that the entire department is set against my secretary and (he, him).

7. That report is no doubt a recommendation with regard to Vincent and (we, us).

8. The Hatchers do not want Terry near their house and (they, them).

9. I think that package is for Nina and (I, me).

10. Grandpa gave tracts of land to Janie and (he, him).

C. Which of the two sentence pairs is correct in each of the following?

1. a. Our small grocery was independent from the large chains.
   b. Our small grocery was independent of the large chains.

2. a. Your attitude is quite different from mine.
   b. Your attitude is quite different than mine.

3. a. I was planning on calling you this week.
   b. I was planning to call you this week.

4. a. Reception duties were divided between Diana, Chris, and Lynn.
   b. Reception duties were divided among Diana, Chris, and Lynn.

5. a. I have no idea where he was at that night.
   b. I have no idea where he was that night.

6. a. We might of tried harder to improve things.
   b. We might have tried harder to improve things.

7. a. The book fell off the shelf and startled us.
   b. The book fell off of the shelf and startled us.

8. a. Did your expectations correspond with reality?
   b. Did your expectations correspond to reality?

9. a. I jumped into the swimming pool without thinking.
   b. I jumped in the swimming pool without thinking.

10. a. Why are you angry with Mona?
    b. Why are you angry at Mona?

11. a. Every record is accompanied with a photograph.
    b. Every record is accompanied by a photograph.

12. a. I am frustrated and angry with my financial difficulties.
    b. I am frustrated and angry at my financial difficulties.

13. a. Sharon was pouring a thick liquid into the jar.
    b. Sharon was pouring a thick liquid in the jar.

Conjunctions

188 Conjunctions are connectors; they join together words, phrases, or clauses. There are three categories of conjunctions: coordinating, subordinating, and correlative.

189 Coordinating conjunctions join together elements of equal rank: nouns with nouns, phrases with phrases, independent clauses with independent clauses, and so on. They do not join independent clauses to dependent clauses because they are not of equal rank. The most common coordinating conjunctions are *and, or, but, nor,* and *for.*

> Mr. Dalli **and** his wife have purchased a huge block of stock. (connects nouns)
> Under the sofa **or** on the braided rug are possible spots where the dog might be sleeping. (connects phrases)
> He longed to receive the scholarship, **but** he had no realistic hope of being awarded it. (connects clauses)

190 Correlative conjunctions also join elements of equal rank, but they differ from coordinating conjunctions in that they are used in pairs. The most common correlatives include the following pairs: *either...or, neither...nor, both...and, not only...but* (or *but also*), and *whether...or.*

> **Either** Carmen **or** Ursula will be elected.
> **Neither** the bookkeeper **nor** the secretary had ever seen those accounts.
> **Not only** were you trying to usurp his power, **but** you were anticipating seizing his position for yourself; isn't that right?

191 Subordinating conjunctions connect dependent clauses to independent clauses. The verb *to subordinate* means to place in a lower rank or position. Thus, the dependent clause (or subordinate clause) is of a lower rank than the independent clause (main clause). The dependent clause functions as a single part of speech—as an adverb, an adjective, or a noun. Some of the most common subordinating conjunctions are *after, although, as, because, before, for, if, once, since, till, unless, until, when, whenever, where,* and *wherever.*

> **After** we walked along the path for a few minutes, Gil decided to sit and rest.
> We had no idea **where** Joann was staying.
> **Unless** there is another reason for delay, we should proceed **whenever** Marsha returns.

Relative pronouns behave like subordinating conjunctions in that they make the clauses they introduce dependent, or subordinate. These pronouns include *that, which, who, what, whoever, whom, whomever,* and *whose.*

The house **that** we hoped to purchase had been on the market only a few days.

Whoever ordered this furniture has to pay delivery charges.

Carol Beri is the student **who** worked in the library last year.

Some subordinating conjunctions are more than one word: *as if, as though, as soon as, even though, in order that, in order to, in that, no matter how, so that.*

As soon as I hear from him, I will inform you of his decision.

Even though we know that you are lying, we will listen to all you have to say.

In order to conclude this matter, you should send payment at once to the above address.

192   Dependent clauses can act as nouns.

Where he lives now is not known by anyone in the firm. (The clause acts as a noun; it is the subject of the sentence.)

He would do the work for **whatever was given to him**. (The clause acts as object of the preposition.)

193   Dependent clauses can act as adjectives.

I wanted to buy a dog **that was small but fluffy**. The book **that I read last week** was frightening.

194   Dependent clauses can act as adverbs.

Whenever I saw him in the shop, I simply didn't go in. Tell us as specifically **as you can recall**.

195   Another category of words could be included in either this section on conjunctions or the section on adverbs. These are conjunctive adverbs (single words) and transitional phrases (more than a single word), which act both as adverbs and as conjunctions. See Tables 2-2 and 2-3 for a list of conjunctive adverbs and transitional phrases. They separate independent clauses and are used after a semicolon or a period, not with a comma. To use a comma would create a run-on.

Correct

We expect to receive a report any moment; **moreover**, we expect the report to contain the information you seek.

There were no signs of habitation; **indeed,** there were no
signs of anyone having been there at all for some time.

They participated in the conference held last month;
nevertheless, they made no real contribution to the
proceedings.

Mr. Sanchez wrote his comments on the report; **in fact,**
he added another page to the back of the report.

Leonora and Victoria have volunteered to assist me; **at the
same time,** they have not seemed interested in the
program.

All of us admired Mr. Kunio and considered him our role
model; **in other words,** he was our mentor.

Acceptable

All of us admired Mr. Kunio and considered him our role
model. In other words, he was our mentor.

Wrong

All of us admired Mr. Kunio and considered him our role
model, in other words, he was our mentor.

Interjections

196   Of the eight parts of speech, the interjection is the one that requires
the least discussion. Interjections are identified easily and offer little
or no difficulty to the CR. Interjections are words that express mild
or strong feeling, and they are followed by either a period or an exclamation point.

> **Oh,** I have no idea what you mean by that question.
> **Wow!** You look fantastic!
> **Phooey!** I left my wallet at home and we have no money
> now.

The decision whether to use a comma or an exclamation point
depends on the emotion conveyed in the speaker's words. The CR
should take care not to overuse the exclamation point, but rather
reserve it for situations that clearly demand its strength.

Interjections can occur within a sentence.

> I hoped to see him again, but, **oh,** I just couldn't go
> through with it.
> Sheila tried to get that promotion, but, **alas,** she was
> passed over for promotion time and again.

Unit Exercise

Use the blank space on this page to list all the underlined words and give their part of speech. If the word is a noun or pronoun, indicate its function in the sentence as well.

There must have been two hundred <u>kids</u> lined up <u>outside</u> the studio. <u>I</u> asked myself why I <u>had</u> bothered to show up—<u>but</u> then I had had occasion to ask myself that question <u>frequently</u>. <u>Oh</u>, I may as well go ahead and stand <u>here</u> endlessly <u>in</u> the burning sun and take my <u>chances</u> like everyone else. So I stood in the <u>line</u>; <u>in fact</u>, I remained while others started leaving. I was exhausted, but I also felt <u>hopeful</u>, especially <u>each</u> time someone <u>left</u> the <u>line</u>. Finally it was my turn to go inside. For <u>me</u>, this was a <u>monumental</u> turning <u>point</u> in my life. I walked <u>boldly</u> <u>into</u> the <u>dark</u> <u>studio</u>. I wished that <u>either</u> Sandra <u>or</u> he could be <u>with</u> me. There were <u>five</u> <u>hopefuls</u> ahead of me. They had the same <u>desperate</u> <u>look</u> on their <u>faces</u> that I knew I was wearing. I felt <u>despondent</u>. The man in charge <u>shot</u> me a disinterested <u>look</u> and then turned <u>his</u> head <u>immediately</u> to speak <u>with</u> someone else. <u>Waiting</u> was killing me. I heard my name, and <u>I</u> began to tremble. I walked to the stage. For <u>me</u>, <u>this</u> was the <u>moment</u> of truth. Either I <u>could</u> give <u>it</u> my best or I could go blank. I didn't <u>know</u> <u>what</u> I would end up doing; <u>moreover</u>, I didn't know how I would manage. Then the <u>oddest</u> <u>thing</u> occurred: I no longer <u>cared</u> what happened in this audition. I didn't <u>care</u> <u>about</u> the part. I forgot <u>my</u> <u>dreams</u>, my <u>ambitions</u>, my <u>career</u>.

3

Punctuation

Because a CR's competency will be judged finally by the quality of his or her transcripts, this unit is likely to become the one referred to most frequently. Whereas Units 1 and 2 are "knowledge" sections, Unit 3 is more utilitarian and lends itself more readily to quick reference.

Punctuation can make or break a transcript. Too much punctuation can disrupt the smooth flow of words for the reader; insufficient or misplaced punctuation can alter or obscure the meaning of the words that were spoken, thereby sabotaging the CR's goal of producing a transcript that will convey to the reader exactly what was said. Thus, it is crucial for the CR to insert punctuation rather than leave it entirely up to the typist or scopist, because the CR was *there*! Editing can be performed afterward, of course, to improve quality, but the CR's understanding, even interpretation, should be the basis for punctuation.

A sound rule to follow is: "When in doubt, don't." Generally speaking, too little punctuation is better than too much.

The guidelines that follow are gramatically sound, although a few may differ from the rules set forth for other professions, such as newspaper journalists. A few may be in dispute within the CR industry—and those are pointed out in most cases—but the CR will of course follow the preferences of his or her employer.

End Punctuation

End punctuation, for the most part, will present comparatively few problems for the CR. The period, question mark, and exclamation point are the primary end, or terminal, punctuation marks, although the dash is sometimes in that position.

197 The Period

- The period is used after a declarative statement.

  The subpoena was delivered yesterday.
  She revealed his name with obvious displeasure.

- The period is used after a mild imperative or a request.

> Have a seat, Miss Richards.
> Would you state your name for the record.

- No period is used when a sentence is interrupted before it can be completed.

> A. The road to the inn was—
> Q. The new or the old road, ma'am?
> A. —not completed at the time. The old one.

- No period is used after items in an enumeration that is not part of a sentence.

> The police dragnet produced the following items:
> 1. a set of playing cards
> 2. an old bicycle
> 3. thirteen suspects

- No period is used after a sentence included within another sentence.

> "I cannot hear you," the man said.
> The jury is an invaluable part of our judicial system—
>   hopefully, you realize that—and you should be proud
>   to participate in it.

- The period is placed inside the end quotation marks.

> Marsha reported the loss by announcing, "It's all over,
>   you know."

Exception: When a special term is set off in single quotation marks and is the last word in the sentence, the single quote goes *inside* the period. This type of sentence would be a rare occurrence for the CR. Otherwise, single quotation marks, like double ones, go outside the period.

> The following are Janice Dawson's exact words: "I
>   asked him to explain what he meant by the term
>   'conspirator'."
> I told Garrett, "You said to her, 'Get out of my
>   house!'"

198   **The Question Mark**

- The most obvious and most frequent use of this mark is, of course, at the end of an interrogative sentence.

> Have you appeared before Judge O'Shea previously?
> Did you see this man in your neighborhood on June
>   13th?

- The question mark is not used with an indirect question.

> I wondered where she went that evening.
> Kim asked Darlene if she had enough money.

- A question mark is used at the end of a declarative sentence if it is obvious, from the speaker's inflection, that the statement is actually meant as a question.

> You are certain of that fact?
> And the car was undamaged?

- Do not use a question mark after a request or a command.

> Will you tell us your profession.
> Will you take a seat now.

> **Note:** Though these requests are stated in question form, the speaker is not really asking for an answer. It would be absurd, for example, to expect an answer to the following: "Will you please state your name." One would not answer, "Yes, I will tell you my name." The anticipated reply would be simply a name.

- A question contained within a declarative statement still retains the question mark.

> What was his motive? was the question on the minds of
>   the jurors.
> Were the two men aware of the embezzlement? is the
>   issue at hand.

- A question mark is placed inside or outside the end quotation mark, depending on the context of the sentence.
  If the entire sentence, including the quoted matter, is a question, then the question mark is placed outside the end quotation mark.

> Can we, as Shakespeare wrote, "defend this emerald
>   isle"?
> Did he say to you, "Let's correct Meggan's wrongs"?

  If only the quoted material is interrogative in nature, the question mark is placed inside the end quotation mark.

> Mr. Terria asked me, "Do you recognize this woman?"
> I asked you, "Where were you that night?"

- Repeat the question mark in a list or series of questions, even incomplete ones.

> Ms. Miller, who was at the meeting? Where was it?
>   When? How long did it last?

Did you see John Hayes? Lee Greer? Carrie Dunn?
You went into town? By car? By bicycle?

- Do not use a question mark with parenthetical elements that occur midsentence and are set off by commas.

   Peg Hayes was, shall we say, our liaison.
   That statement is, wouldn't you agree, somewhat exaggerated.

- When testimony is quoted during proceedings, it can be handled as follows:

   Q. Did you previously testify as follows: "Question: Did you know Marie Carrier? Answer: No, I never met her"?

   Note: No period is used after "her."

- A question inserted in the middle of a sentence and set off by dashes is followed by a question mark.

   My agent was—oh, what was her name?—Mary Norton.
   I just want to tell everyone—can you all hear me?—how happy I was to see my husband return.

- Questions that follow a colon, if complete sentences, begin with a capital.

   The question is as follows: Do you remember seeing Richard Palmer on Sunday, May 18th?
   What I need to know is just this: Where were you on the night Linn Yeats died?

- Some statements that appear at first glance to be questions actually are not. The CR should avoid using question marks with such sentences.

   He asked how am I doing.
   When you inquired how's Joy been feeling, I couldn't reply.

199   The Exclamation Point

The exclamation point is used to express strong feeling. The CR should be careful to use it only when the speaker's voice clearly indicates that it is appropriate.

- The exclamation point is used after a clearly exclamatory statement.

   The entire family was murdered!
   I was so completely thrilled!

- Use an exclamation point after an interjection of strong feeling.

> Drat! He escaped.
> Wow! Eighteen of us were present.

- Like the question mark, the exclamation point may be placed inside or outside the end quotation mark, depending on the context of the sentence.

  If the entire sentence can be interpreted as exclamatory, or very strong in feeling, the exclamation point goes outside the end quotation mark.

> To my shock, Ellis told me, "Jan wants to see you"!
> After so many months of the store's being closed, the
> sign on the door reads, "Open"!

  If only the quoted material is exclamatory, the exclamation point goes inside the end quotation mark.

> She told me that he exclaimed, "Kill the judge!"
> I clearly heard the child shout, "Please help me!"

- An exclamation point may follow an imperative statement, but only one that conveys strong feeling.

> Hand me that right now!
> Do exactly as I say!

- When a parenthetical is set off midsentence by dashes and it is exclamatory, the exclamation point should be placed before the final dash.

> He turned to me—I couldn't believe what I was see-
> ing!—and I saw the cut slashed down from his
> temple to his chin.
> We walked into that house—it was a nightmare!—and
> discovered the bodies of the two men.

200   Multiple Punctuation Marks

Except with quotation marks and dashes, two punctuation marks are not used at the same place in a sentence. In situations where it might seem appropriate for two marks to be used, use only the one that is stronger.

> Who screamed out, "This building is on fire!"

In the above sentence, one might be tempted to use a question mark at the end of the sentence in addition to the other marks. However, this should not be done. The exclamation mark is used here because it is judged to be stronger than the question mark. But note that the following is also acceptable.

Who screamed out, "This building is on fire"?

Wrong

Who screamed out, "This building is on fire!"?

201 The Dash as Final Punctuation

If a sentence is obviously not completed, the dash is the final mark of punctuation.

Q. When did you last see him?
A. It was way back when—
Q. Give us a date, please.

202 The Ellipsis as Final Punctuation

It would be a rare situation in which a CR would use an ellipsis as final punctuation. Use a dash, not an ellipsis, to indicate that the speaker was interrupted or trailed off. When a passage is being quoted verbatim, and the person quoting says, "Dot dot dot," then an ellipsis would be used in the place where the dots are read.

Your statement, Mrs. Hughes, was, "I never saw Ellen DeVille prior to that night . . ."

In such a case, the ellipsis does not indicate an interruption or trailing-off speech, but rather indicates that the quote is not being read in its entirety.

Exercise

Punctuate the following sentences.

1. He inquired of me Where did you place the records

2. We heard a rumor and I think it was totally unfounded that you were planning to leave

3. What did he tell you is important for me to know

4. Would you please state your name and address

5. I cannot stand this another moment

6. My sister looked at me I could have died and wept

7. I wrote in my letter to her Were you aware of this problem

8. Oh I thought this was Ms. Tibble's office

9. Can you believe that she answered, Yes

10. Mother always asked if we're hungry

11. Did you say to him You don't even know the meaning of the word 'disheartened'

12. Can you describe his face his clothes his physical size

13. Father was didn't you know a difficult man to deal with

14. Where did he go that night was my question

Parentheses

CRs use parentheses not in the traditional manner (for asides and parenthetical material) but in a way exclusive to the CR profession. They are used to describe actions that are crucial to an understanding of what transpired in the courtroom; they do not record words actually spoken.

203 Parentheses are used to describe physical actions.

Q. Did you see him before that day?
A. (The witness nodded her head.)

Q. Are you feeling all right, Mr. Carrio?
A. I—yes—no— (The witness slumped over in his chair, unconscious.)

204 Verbal occurrences in the courtroom that are not taken down verbatim by the CR can be noted in parentheses.

(The reporter read the last question.)
(There was an off-the-record discussion.)

205 Parentheses are used to indicate recesses and adjournments.

(Court was adjourned at 5:15 p.m.)
(A recess was taken at 9:45 a.m.)

206 Within the parentheses, punctuation should be just as it would be if it were written without parentheses. The material within the parentheses should be a complete sentence.

207 **Enumerations**

Parentheses are used to enclose numbers or letters used in lists or enumerations.

I understand that he told you several things: (1) that your father had been in an accident; (2) that your mother could not be located; (3) that your father was in West County General Hospital in critical condition.

We will take a look at (a) Samuel Pammen's criminal record, (b) his work history, (c) his personal reputation, and (d) his psychological profile as prepared by Dr. Tonbee.

Note: If the words used by the speaker are "first," "second," etc., the CR may elect to write out the words in the transcript. If the speaker enumerates by saying "one," "two," etc., the CR should use numerals in parentheses. (See the discussion of formatting in Unit 10.)

Quotation Marks

When and where to use quotation marks can be a tricky issue for the CR. There will be times when the CR will have considerable difficulty discerning the exact point at which a quotation begins and ends, or, indeed, that there is a quotation at all. Of course, if the speaker is reading from a document, it is obvious that the material being presented is also being quoted; however, many situations encountered by the CR will not be nearly so obvious.

The following guidelines are intended to assist the CR in handling the sticky issue of direct quotations. One should always remember to be conservative and to use quotation marks only when the material is being quoted verbatim.

208   A period is placed inside the end quotation mark, whether double or single.

> Jane was a boastful person. Her favorite line—and she said this all of the time—was, "Every single day and in every way I am getting better and better."
> I am reading from the letter Ray wrote to me. He wrote, "I wish Kit hadn't said to me, 'It is now completely over.'"

Note: The only exception to this rule, as noted earlier, occurs when a technical or special term in single quotation marks falls at the end of the sentence.

> Merle's exact words were, "I govern my life according to the principles of 'Deism'."

209   A comma also is placed inside the end quotation mark.

> "Shakespeare is a second-rate poet," she wrote in her paper.

Sierra nodded at me and said, "False accusations cannot be proved," and then she walked away.

210   Always place a semicolon outside the end quotation mark. The CR will have infrequent uses for the semicolon in conjunction with quotation marks, but it is important to know how to handle such situations if they do indeed occur.

> The director said, "Not another penny for that cause"; indeed, he is known for his cheapness.
> Mother announced to the family, "We will be moving to Wisconsin"; moreover, she allowed no discussion from anyone.

211   A colon also is placed outside the end quotation mark. This too will probably be an infrequent occurrence.

> "We shall overcome our productivity losses": this is a typically American viewpoint.
> Doris demanded, "Tell me where my daughter is": that is all she said to me.

212   A question mark is placed either inside or outside the end quotation mark, depending on the content of the sentence.

- If the entire sentence, including the quoted material, is a question, the question mark should be placed outside the end quotation mark.

> Did Josephine say to Ellis, "I am going away for a few days"?
> Did the letter end with his statement, "I am forever in your debt"?

- If only the quoted material is a question, then the question mark is placed inside the end quotation mark.

> Nancy asked with great emotion, "What use to the world am I?"
> He looked at me and asked, "Why did you do that to Lucy?"

213   The exclamation point follows the same rule as the question mark; that is, it may be placed inside or outside the end quotation mark, depending on the meaning of the sentence.

- If the entire sentence, including the quoted material, is exclamatory in nature, the exclamation point is placed outside the end quotation mark.

I actually heard Earl say to Shala, "You're not welcome here"!

Ms. Lange told Lauren, "Peter is not your brother"!

- If only the quoted material is exclamatory in nature, then the exclamation point is placed inside the end quotation mark.

It is obvious that "Patriotism forever!" doesn't incite the crowds as it once might have.

The child screamed, "Grady's hurting me!" so often that no one paid much attention to her wails.

214   Split quotations are handled by setting off the interrupting words (for example, words like *he said* and *he replied*) with commas. The second part of the split does not begin with a capital letter unless it is a proper noun or adjective or the pronoun *I*.

"There was no other way to handle the problem," the woman sobbed, "except to confront Miss Sullivan."

"Rita purchased everything on the list," Fred told me, "Cuban cigars being the only exception."

215   Do not use quotation marks with indirect quotes.

He asked me if I had decided to accompany Andrea.

They told me that David has been seriously ill for the past two weeks.

Note: The above sentence, if it were a direct quotation, would read as follows:

They told me, "David has been seriously ill for the past two weeks."

216   It is frequently impossible to distinguish between a verbatim quote and an indirect quotation.

He said, "Sure."

OR: He said sure.

I told Emory, "We weren't ready to leave when Gil arrived."

OR: I told Emory we weren't ready to leave when Gil arrived.

Q. What did you tell your father?

A. I told him everything's just fine.

OR: A. I told him, "Everything's just fine."

Q. What did you say when he asked you to spy for him?

A. I said, "No."

Or: A. I said no.

In the above sentence pairs, the inclusion or omission of quotation marks makes no distinguishable difference in meaning. In the sentences that *do* use quotation marks, there is no clear indication that the words are being quoted verbatim. Omitting the quotes would make no difference. However, this often is not the case. The omission or inclusion of quotation marks can indeed affect the meaning conveyed to the reader. Because the CR should have in mind at all times rendering to the reader what really happened and what was actually meant, the CR will have to make some difficult decisions regarding quotations. Some CRs use quotation marks sparingly and only when they cannot avoid doing so. However, quotation marks can be useful in producing an accurate transcript, despite their difficulty and ambiguity at times.

217 The CR often will be able to tell whether a direct quote is present or not by the content of the transcript, that is, by considering what is said before and after the section in question.

Q. What did your brother say about James Fields?

A. He said, "He's behaving very strangely."

In the sentence above, the second *he* obviously refers to James Fields; there is no confusion possible. With or without the quotation marks, the meaning is the same. However, consider the following:

Q. What did your brother say about his own physical condition?

A. He said he's been feeling much better recently.

In the sentence above, insertion of quotation marks would change the meaning of the sentence. Notice the change in the sentence below:

A. He said, "He's been feeling much better recently."

The addition of the quotation marks indicates that *he's* refers to someone other than the speaker. Obviously such an interpretation would be erroneous, given the content of the question.

218 Rambling constructions that contain some quoted and some non-quoted statements can be rendered most easily understood by using quotation marks, even when they are not absolutely necessary. Note the difference in readability between the following passage with and without the quotation marks.

I was planning to say to Dave I want a divorce, but then he came home with his brother, so I didn't want to say that to him, not with Ken there. Instead, I said I am going to my sister's for a while, because I thought that way he would agree and it wouldn't be as awkward. Dave said sure, go ahead and go. When are you coming back? I said I didn't know. Then Dave's face turned red, and I knew trouble was coming. Dave started shouting come here, right now, and I started toward the door. Ken said to Dave to let me go, but Dave said no way.

The above passage is understandable as it stands, but reading is smoother with the quotation marks inserted.

I was planning to say to Dave, "I want a divorce," but then he came home with his brother, so I didn't want to say that to him, not with Ken there. Instead, I said, "I am going to my sister's for a while," because I thought that way he would agree and it wouldn't be as awkward. Dave said, "Sure, go ahead and go. When are you coming back?" I said I didn't know. Then Dave's face turned red, and I knew trouble was coming. Dave started shouting, "Come here, right now!" and I started toward the door. Ken said to Dave to let me go, but Dave said, "No way!"

219   Sentences with personal pronouns can cause tremendous confusion, as the presence or absence of quotation marks can completely change the meaning.

Q. Did you tell Joseph, "You took the money"?

Or:

Q. Did you tell Joseph you took the money?

Obviously, the first version is saying that Joseph took the money, whereas the second version is saying that the speaker took the money. Usually, the content of the transcript will make it obvious to the CR which version is the correct one. If this is not the case, and the CR cannot decide, the sentence can be written in a third, rather noncommittal manner.

Q. Did you tell Joseph, you took the money?

220   Sometimes doubt is cleared instantly by the speaker's use of the word "quote" and sometimes "end-quote." If this occurs, the CR knows exactly where to insert the quotation marks. Do not, however, actually write in the word "quote" unless it is part of a phrase or clause that precedes that quote, as in the second example below:

Q. What did she say in her letter to you dated January 5, 1984?
A. She said, and I am reading directly from the letter itself, "I intend to leave you everything when I die."

Q. What did Mr. Boswell say to you and Donna Pietra?
A. He said, and I quote, "The two of you will be promoted to floor supervisors."

Q. Those are his exact words, then?
A. Yes, exact words.

Q. And what did you reply?
A. I said I was looking forward to the opportunity.

221   If it is clear where a quotation begins but the CR cannot fathom where the quotation ends, the CR can omit the quotation marks, using a capital letter preceded by a comma to show where the quotation begins and leaving out any indication of where it ends. It is preferable not to have to do this, of course, but it may be the only solution.

Q. What did the man say to you?
A. He said, You had better hand over that wallet, if you can understand what that means.

The question is whether the quote ends after *wallet* or after *means*. This is one way to handle this uncomfortable and bewildering situation; however, if your employer prefers another way of handling it, follow your firm's preferred method.

222   Quoted phrases, terms, and fragments of quoted material are set off with quotation marks.

> The newspaper article called the defendant a "hideous monster of a man."
> "To be or not to be" was his favorite line.

223   Technical terms, that is, terms not widely understood by the general public, can be set off with quotation marks, but this practice should not be overdone. For example, in a maritime case, a multitude of maritime terms will inevitably be used, but these should not all be set off with quotation marks. To do so would "dot" the transcript and wear out the CR. Only terms that are odd or unique to the case should be set off.

> The editor was expecting to receive the "blues" that day.
>   (a publishing term)
> The WASP was ordered for storing digits in the computer.

224   Titles of various works, both short and long, are enclosed in quotation marks. Many, such as book titles, are traditionally underlined to indicate that they are to be italicized in print, but the CR uses quotes in place of underlining. There is only one exception: court cases, which are underlined by most CRs (though not all). Use quotation marks to enclose the titles of the following:

> short stories
> poems and poetry collections
> essays
> plays
> magazines
> pamphlets and periodicals
> movies
> television programs, both series titles and specific episodes
> songs
> books
> newspapers and tabloids
> articles
> radio shows
> titles of chapters or parts of a book
> reports
> works of art (statues, paintings, sculptures)
> names of trains, planes, ships, boats

> The public relations officer is writing a pamphlet entitled "Knowing Your Company," and it contains sections such as "Insurance Benefits" and "Annual and Sick Leave."
> Did the band play "The Man on the Flying Trapeze"?
> We rode the train called "The Crescent" down to New Orleans.
> The statue on display is called "Appeal to the Great Spirit."
> Reruns of "I Love Lucy" can still be seen on weekday mornings.

225   Foreign terms that are unfamiliar to the general public should be enclosed in quotation marks. Conversely, foreign words or terms that have become commonplace should not be set off.

> He spends about $5,500 per annum on his automobiles.
> The Court's verdict is not, per se, a judgment for the government.

His "mal à la tête" was his common complaint.

He was a practitioner of "feng-shui," which I think is a form of magic.

226 If an English translation of a foreign term is contained within a sentence, it too should be placed in quotation marks.

"Angst" can be translated as "anxiety," although it is not an exact translation.

He suffered from "ennui"–"boredom"–most of his life.

227 Do not use quotation marks with names of diseases or technical words in general use.

He died of carbon monoxide poisoning.

The prescription was for penicillin, not for erythromycin.

His arthritic condition rendered him immobile.

Infectious mononucleosis is highly contagious, isn't it?

228 When dealing with words in their roles as words, quotation marks are used. These are introduced by expressions such as *the term, the expression, the word(s)*, and *known as*. When the expression *so-called* introduces a word or phrase, quotation marks are not necessary, but the CR may choose to use them.

The term "conclusion" does not have the same literary color as does the word "denouement."

The expression "serious money" is best used to describe amounts that are larger than that!

The phrase "driving me to distraction" predates psychological researchers.

The quotation marks are used only for the first occurrence of the term or word, not every occurrence.

Note: Some terms are used repeatedly in courtroom sessions, and the CR would be justified, perhaps advised, not to use quotation marks with such stock phrases.

The term preponderance of the evidence means simply the greater weight of the evidence.

The word negligence implies lack of ordinary care and prudence.

229 Slang terms or words used in a special sense may be enclosed in quotation marks.

I told Harry he could not expect to get a "freebie" from
me.
I tried to get him to "chill out" but no use.
Poor Kevin was such a "goober."

Note: Be careful not to overuse quotation marks for this kind of
material.

230   Nicknames are sometimes set off in quotation marks.

Cary "Antelope" Barrios is our star basketball player.
Eldon "Egghead" Wilson will debate Luis "Blockhead"
Thimes; so who do you think will win?

231   Short quotations are introduced by a comma; long quotations are introduced by a colon. Quotations of several lines (usually ten or more) may
be single-spaced and indented an additional ten spaces on each side.
CRs who prefer to avoid single-spacing may indent long quotations
five spaces on both sides and retain double-spacing. A third method
is to set the quotation like regular text, starting each paragraph of
quoted material with a quotation mark and using the end quotation
mark only at the end of the final paragraph of the quotation.

232   Letters and numbers written *as* numbers or letters, and so labeled, are
enclosed in quotation marks.

The letter "r" often has new meaning when used in
programming.
The letter "d" sometimes looks like the number "8" when
written hurriedly.

233   Irony or sarcasm may be denoted with quotation marks, but the CR
should use this method quite sparingly, if ever.

Q. How would you describe his treatment of Carmen?
A. Oh, he was a real "sweetheart" all right. He beat her up a couple
of times a month or more. He couldn't hold a job. Yes, he was a
"darling."

234   A CR may, on rare occasions, have to quote poetry. Lines of poetry
in a transcript are usually not set line for line but run in, with a slash
(virgule) between lines. Like other quoted material, poetry is set off by
quotation marks.

As the poet said, "Love can only flourish in the hearts of
the enlightened."

"Or I shall live your epitaph to make, / Or you survive
when I in earth am rotten."

Excessive use of quotation marks, or use without sound cause, can ruin the physical appearance and smooth reading of a transcript. Such abuse can also, more seriously, change the meaning of what was spoken. Thus, the CR should give special consideration to when and how to use this particular mark of punctuation.

Exercises

A. Insert quotation marks where necessary. Some changes in punctuation and capitalization may also be needed.

Q. What did he say to you?

A. He said I can be influenced.

Q. Was that his exact word—influenced?

A. Yes, that's what he said. Then he winked.

Q. How did you respond?

A. Thanks but no thanks I said.

Q. Didn't you ask him what do you mean by that?

A. No. I said I knew what he meant.

Q. Was that the end of the conversation?

A. That day, yes.

Q. You had a subsequent conversation?

A. The next night I went to see The Shooting Party at the Star Cinema. I was going with my friend Susan Josef, whom I call Winky.

Q. You saw Mr. Alexander there?

A. I saw him afterward. We were at a coffee shop and he walked in. He walked over to my table and said he wanted to speak to me for a minute.

Q. What did you say then?

A. I said okay.

Q. And then what happened?

A. He said he was desperate. He needed my help.

Q. Did he explain?

A. He said I need your help. There's no one else I can turn to now. Then, let me think, oh, he started crying and saying please, please, don't turn away. He just kept repeating that. I wanted to get away from him. I never liked him or trusted him, but he was out of control by that time. I finally told him to please stop it. He didn't stop, though.

Q. What did you do?

A. I started walking away. I walked toward the bus stop.

Q. So you were outside the coffee shop?

A. Yes. He and I had walked outside to talk.

Q. You left your friend?

A. Yes, I did. I was frightened and just wanted to get away, and I forgot all about her. He ran after me shouting you little tramp, come back here right now!

Q. Did you answer him?

A. No. I ran into an apartment building where I knew there was a pay phone. I called my brother and told him where I was and please come pick me up, Andy, I said.

Q. What did Andy say?

A. He said he was on his way. Stay where you are and scream for help if you need to he told me.

Q. Didn't you have a job for the next day?

A. Yes. I had a small part in a movie, just a few lines, but it was in a movie called Over Yonder From Whence We Came.

Q. Had you appeared in any other movies?

A. Just one—Riverton Smith and Unger Black was the name of it. It wasn't much of a movie. But I've been on a couple of TV shows— The Carol Burns Hour and Try Your Luck.

Q. Back to that night. Did your brother arrive?

A. Not before Alexander found me. He grabbed me by the arm—I thought he'd break it— and pulled me into an alley. He threatened to cut a big X across my face for abandoning him.

B. Correct any improperly used quotation marks and insert any that have been omitted. Punctuation and capitalization may also need to be altered.

Q. Did you say to Zachary you didn't do that correctly?

A. No. I said I didn't know if I had done it properly or not.

Q. Did you tell him it's your fault?

A. No, I didn't. I said, "The report was his responsibility, and he didn't do any supervision at all." I felt that if I hadn't done it properly, it was partly his fault.

Q. Did he agree with your evaluation?

A. He said, "Nothing."

Q. He refused to discuss it; is that what you're saying?

A. Yes.

Q. What report was this?

A. The new personnel manual entitled This Is Your Firm!

Q. Did you write the entire manual?

A. Everything except the section called Medical and Dental.

Q. Who wrote that section?

A. My so-called supervisor.

Q. Did Zachary ever answer any of your questions.

A. He was perpetually, as his secretary always told me, unavailable. He did write me a note, however, which I couldn't even read. I can't distinguish his m from his n or his a from his o. His numbers are worse. A 3 looks like a 5 or an 8 and a 1 looks just like a 7. It was a fiasco. I took it to him and said would you like to interpret this for me.

Q. What did he say to that?

A. He said, "That was my problem, not his."

The Apostrophe

The apostrophe has three primary uses: (1) in contractions, (2) in possessives, and (3) in unusual plurals and verbs. The contraction is one of the less difficult marks of punctuation and should give the CR little trouble.

235   **Contractions**

The apostrophe indicates the omission of letters in words that are written as contractions. Although contractions are frowned on in formal writing, the CR can hardly avoid them in oral testimony.

Q. The hearing is scheduled for two o'clock this afternoon; is that right?
A. There's nothing in the subpoena that would determine that.

Q. I can't believe that you didn't hear anything. Are you quite sure you shouldn't change your testimony?
A. I'll change nothing.

Note: o'clock (of the clock), *there's* (there is), *can't* (cannot), *didn't* (did not), *shouldn't* (should not), *I'll* (I shall or I will).

236   The apostrophe can indicate the omission of numerals.

Q. Was the appeal filed in the early '70s or was it in '69?
A. It was filed in '71.

Note: The number *19* has been omitted from the years in the above sentences.

237   **Possessives**

Most singular possessives are formed by adding an apostrophe and an *s.*

The judge's decision was overthrown today.
The clerk's error cost us a day's proceedings.

Note: An alternate form of the possessive uses the word *of* instead of an *'s.*

The decision of the judge was overthrown today.
The error of the clerk cost us the proceedings of a day.

238   Singular nouns that end with an *s* can be put in the possessive form by adding an apostrophe only (*James' decision*) or by adding both an apostrophe and an *s* (*James's decision*). Some strongly prefer just the addition of the apostrophe in such cases; others follow this rule: If there is an extra final *s* sound *spoken* in the possessive form, then the *'s* should be used (pronunciation would be "*Jameses*").

Ross' sedan was stolen last night and he doesn't expect to recover it.
Tess' hair is the envy of all the girls in her school.

Or:

Ross's sedan was stolen last night and he doesn't expect to recover it.
Tess's hair is the envy of all the girls in her school.

Consistency is important; the CR should establish a preference and stick with it throughout a transcript.

239   The apostrophe is never used for possessives of personal pronouns (*my, mine, your, yours, our, ours, its, hers, theirs, their, whose, his*).

Q. Was the car theirs until last May?
A. I'm not sure whose it was. Maybe it was his, but I know it wasn't hers.

> Was ours the only flight delayed by the blizzard? Joe said
> that it's a long wait to find its number.

240   A frequent source of confusion for CRs (and a lot of other people!) is the difference between *whose* (possessive form) and *who's* (contraction of *who is*); between *its* (possessive) and *it's* (contraction of *it is*); and between *your* (possessive) and *you're* (contraction of *you are*).

Q. You say the scheme against them wasn't your idea; **whose** was it?
A. I don't know **who's** responsible.

Q. The puppy hurt **its** foot when Meg dropped it.
A. **It's** too bad this happened.

Q. **You're** being difficult. Now tell us, what was **your** exact statement?
A. I don't recall.

241   Plural possessives that end with *s* are formed by adding an apostrophe.

> The boys' jackets were left at school.
> Five students' scores were lower than last year.

242   Some plurals do not end with *s*. These are made possessive by adding both an apostrophe and an *s* to the end of the word, just as one would form the possessive of a singular word.

> The children's toys were all over the floor.
> The oxen's physical condition was deplorable.

243   The singular and the plural forms of words often sound exactly the same. In practice, the CR must distinguish what form is correct, and this is done by examining the context of the transcript.

244   In forming plural possessives, it is essential that the CR first know how to form plurals! When in doubt, consult your dictionary.

245   To form the singular possessive of a compound word, add an apostrophe and an *s* to the last word in the compound construction.

> The commander-in-chief's orders came to us last night.
> Stratford-on-Avon's memorial to Shakespeare attracts
>   countless tourists.
> My father-in-law's business is thriving.

246 Possessives of word groups are formed by adding the apostrophe and *s* to the last word of that word group.

Three Boys Who Cook's food is better than you'd expect.
Crusaders Club of Smithville's funds were depleted by the gala event.

247 ## Joint vs. Individual Ownership

- Joint ownership is indicated by adding an *'s* to the last name of the group.

Phil and Ramon's grocery has never been robbed in its 27 years of operation.
Carmen and Marie's Chrysler uses more gas than does their Toyota.

Note: In both the examples, a single object is owned by two persons.

- Individual ownership is indicated with *'s* added to each name.

Phil's and Ramon's groceries have never been robbed.
Carmen's and Marie's Chryslers use more gas than does my car.

Note: The plurals *groceries* and *Chryslers* indicate that each member of the two pairs is an individual owner.

- Sometimes common sense will tell the CR that joint ownership is illogical. It would be unlikely, for example, for two or more people to own, say, a toothbrush or a pair of shoes jointly.

Correct

Joe's and Peter's shoes were found in the wooded area behind the cabin.

Wrong

Joe and Peter's shoes were found in the wooded area behind the cabin.

248 For names of periodicals, organizations, etc., the CR should defer to the organization's actual practice.

"Reader's Digest" (not "Readers' Digest")
People's Republic of China
Johnson's Used Cars
National Shorthand Reporters Association

249 To form the possessive of certain singular nouns that end with *ce* or *ss*, some follow a tradition of using an apostrophe only, not an apostrophe and an *s*. The CR may elect to ignore this tradition or follow it.

> For my conscience' sake, I made the confession.
>   (OR: conscience's)
> Justice' cause is best served through a trial by jury.
>   (OR: Justice's)

250 **Double Possessives**

The word *of* indicates possession (*the home of Melinda Zerba*) as does the regular possessive form (*Melinda Zerba's home*). A double possessive makes use of both of these forms of possession.

> That house of Melinda Zerba's is quite a sight, isn't it?
> The frilly dress of Millie Pardue's was the talk of the party.

Note the difference in meaning between the following two sentences:

> That photo of Mimi was blurred.
> That photo of Mimi's was blurred.

The first example is discussing a photograph of Mimi; the second example discusses a photo that belongs to Mimi, which may or may not be a photograph of Mimi herself. Thus, care must be taken in dealing with double possessives, as meaning conceivably can be altered through misuse.

251 Inanimates can be rendered possessive through the use of an apostrophe and an *s*.

> A year's lease was requested by the tenants, although the
>   landlord was pushing for a longer lease of two or three
>   years' duration.
> The check was for two weeks' salary.
> The plane's motor was damaged beyond repair.

Note: Do not confuse possessives and adjectives.

Correct

> Our sales manager resigned.

Wrong

> Our sale's manager resigned.
> Our sales' manager resigned.

252   Unusual Plurals

The plurals of letters, abbreviations, symbols, and figures can be formed by using an apostrophe and an *s*.

> I couldn't tell his o's from his s's.
> Nearly half of the degrees awarded yesterday, surprisingly, were Ph.D.'s.

If no confusion results, the apostrophe can be omitted in forming plurals of this type.

> During the 1960s campus demonstrations were common. (PREFERRED TO 1960's)
> The three-year-old boy recited his ABCs accurately.
> His Ps look like Ts to me. (OR P's and T's)

Use an apostrophe if omitting it might confuse the reader.

> Your on's look like an's. (to avoid the odd-looking *ons* and *ans*)
> He prints his I's but uses script otherwise. (Without the apostrophe, the word looks like another word—*Is*.)

253

Certain verb forms can be created by using an apostrophe and the letter *d* to put a verb in its past tense.

> He X'd out his name from the list.
> The boxer was ko'd in the first round.

Exercises

A. For the following list of words, write first the singular possessive form and then the plural possessive form.

	Singular Possessive	Plural Possessive
child		
week		
lady		
man		
puppy		
mother-in-law		

student

_____

piano

_____

turkey

_____

building

_____

chief

_____

window

_____

scissors

_____

deer

_____

tooth

_____

aunt

_____

dinner

_____

movie

_____

monkey

_____

moss

_____

foot

_____

managing editor

_____

B. Select and underline the correct word for each sentence.

1. I have no idea (whose, who's) going to be elected to office.

2. I don't think (your, you're) grasping the meaning of what I have said.

3. I asked (whose, who's) keys they were, but no one replied.

4. The dog was biting (it's, its) skin relentlessly because of allergies.

5. Do you know (who's, whose) responsible for sending out the invoices at the end of the month?

6. I think (it's, its) going to be a long time before he comes back to this town.

7. (It's, Its) been several years since we were associated with that firm.

8. Have you turned in (your, you're) report to the sales manager?

9. I don't think (it's, its) going to be hard to learn.

10. We couldn't figure out (who's, whose) been tampering with the books.

The Colon

The colon is the punctuation mark of anticipation. It introduces or announces that something is about to follow, something worthy of attention. It marks a break stronger than a comma would indicate, but less strong than the break indicated by a period; and it differs from the semicolon because of its introductory nature.

254   The colon introduces a list that is preceded by words such as *the following* or *as follows*.

> The following sections will be reviewed: 101B, 3124B, 99F, and 831D.
>
> He wrote in his report as follows: "The company is suffering from a marked decline in sales, especially in the Northeast Sector. The other sectors are doing less business than in previous years, the sole exception being the Gulf Sector."

255   When *the following* is part of a question, use a question mark, not a colon.

> You were asked those questions, and did you answer in the following manner?
>
> You had not seen him in five years, and did you write him as follows?

256   If another sentence (or sentences) falls between the introducing statement and the list, no colon is used.

> At the meeting the items discussed were as follows. The first two items received the most attention.
> 1. The annual stockholders' meeting
> 2. Membership drive for next year
> 3. National convention agenda
> 4. Committee on Aging

257   A colon can be used to introduce a short list within a sentence.

> She is taking three courses: English, biology, and French.
> Bob purchased two items: a disk drive and a printer.

If the sentence continues after the list, do not use the colon. Use a dash instead on both sides of the list.

> She is taking three courses — English, biology, and French — and will take three more courses in the spring.

Bob purchased two items—a disk drive and a printer—with his new credit line.

If the sentence is inverted, a colon can still be used.

English, biology, and French: these are the courses she is taking.
A disk drive and a printer: these are the items Bob bought with his new credit line.

Acceptable

English, biology, and French—these are the courses she is taking.
A disk drive and a printer—Bob bought these with his new credit line.

258   A colon introduces extracts, formal statements, and legal documents.

The applicable law here is Civil Code 13, which reads in part: "Any alteration of the certificate is an act of fiscal piracy."
I read from the record: "And on what basis did you act, Miss Kennedy?"

259   Use a colon with the speaker's greeting to her or his audience (direct address).

Mr. Speaker: Ladies and Gentlemen of the Jury:
Mr. President:

Note: When using the colon after direct address, the text that follows should be indented as a new paragraph. If the direct address or greeting is incorporated into the first paragraph, a comma should be used in place of the colon.

260   Use a colon to focus the reader's attention on what follows.

My question is simple: Were you there or not?
There is one issue that we must resolve: Is the defendant guilty or not guilty of the crime?

261   With introductory words such as *namely, for instance, for example,* and *that is,* use a comma, not a colon, unless what follows is a complete sentence.

Correct

She asked for three items: namely, she demanded a red pen, a ruler, and a piece of burlap.

Avoid

She asked for three items: namely, a pen, a ruler, and a piece of burlap.

Correct

She asked for three items, namely, a pen, a ruler, and a piece of burlap.

262   Use a colon to introduce long quotations.

The president of the company addressed his employees by asking: "What are we hoping to achieve? Why are we here? Do we have definite goals outlined? Have you set your priorities for the coming year?"

263   A colon may introduce an appositive in certain constructions.

She had one goal: stardom.

Acceptable

She had one goal—stardom.

The attorney questioned him on two topics: finances and ethics.

Acceptable

The attorney questioned him on two topics—finances and ethics.

Note: In a different construction, commas would be used.

The two topics under discussion, finances and ethics, were discussed by the attorney and his client.

264   Do not use a colon where it is not necessary. For example, a colon should not be used in a sentence containing a short list introduced by *were* or *are*.

Correct

The persons present were Ms. Jones, Miss Lennox, Mrs. Petersen, and Mr. Baker.

Avoid

The persons present were: Ms. Jones, Miss Lennox, Mrs. Petersen, and Mr. Baker.

Preferred

The committee studied various community problems, such as poverty, urban crime, unemployment, and welfare fraud.

Our problems at present are the rent, the utilities, and paying off that old loan.

BUT: Your instructions are: (1) do your homework; (2) clean the kitchen, bathroom, hall, and den; (3) take the dog for a walk.

265 The CR employs the colon to designate speakers in colloquy and for swearing in witnesses.

CROSS EXAMINATION BY MR. HORACE:
By Mr. Horace:
The above-named witness, after having been duly sworn, testified as follows:

Note: Most firms do not use the colon after Q and A, but rather use nothing at all or a period. Use the preference of your firm.

266 With certain introductory phrases and clauses, a colon offers greater clarity than other marks of punctuation.

So that I make myself perfectly clear, Mr. Purcell: Were you or were you not employed by Smith Company on May 10, 1985?

Tell me, Mr. Russell, this one thing: Where were you that evening?

So that we may move forward with this examination: Tell us how you met Frank Yarrow.

In order to facilitate these proceedings: Do you understand the question?

Before we proceed: Are you aware of the time?

267 When a second sentence amplifies, clarifies, or explains the first one, a colon can be used. Note that the first word of the sentence following the colon is uppercased.

I told you several times where I was: I was at the movies.

The officer grimaced when I filed the report: She, too, had been a victim of that crime.

You know you were far closer than mere acquaintances: You were and are intimate friends.

You said that he was rude and arrogant: What did you mean by that?

268   When a question is stated awkwardly, and two questions or statements are related, a colon can clarify what is meant.

> We tried to call out to him, but all we did was: We caused a big commotion.

Acceptable

> We tried to call out to him, but all we did was, we caused a big commotion.

Preferred

> The only things he wanted to know were: Did we know David Marx and when had we last seen him.

Acceptable

> The only things he wanted to know were, did we know David Marx and when had we last seen him.

Preferred

> Perhaps you will remember that her reason is: All through the winter there were problems with the heating system.

Acceptable

> Perhaps you will remember that her reason is, all through the winter there were problems with the heating system.

269   Hours and minutes are set off from each other in written references to time through the use of the colon.

> She asked the tutor to meet her at 10:45 a.m.

270   Certain reference materials employ the colon to distinguish between volume and page numbers, chapter and verse.

> She cited research material gleaned from "The New England Journal of Medicine" 25:108-114.
> Please read the biblical passage I assigned to you, which was from Genesis 2:11.

The Semicolon

The semicolon lies approximately midway between the comma and the period in terms of strength. It can act as either a weak period or a strong comma. This chameleon of punctuation can change to meet the requirements of the sentence, but knowing when to use the semicolon instead of the comma or the period can be tricky and must be a learned skill. The CR should make it a rule never to employ this mark without a sound reason. If properly used, the semicolon can clarify meaning and make reading an easier task.

271   A semicolon can replace a period when the following occur:

- Two sentences are closely related in thought.

- They are not connected by a coordinating conjunction.

- They are somewhat brief.

> Working hard can be satisfying; making money is more satisfying.
> We looked for Baxter; we looked everywhere.

> *Note:* A period could be used instead of the semicolon in the above examples, but it is a somewhat poorer choice because the semicolon indicates the close relationship between the two sentences. On the other hand, a comma would be incorrect; written with a comma the examples would be run-on sentences.

272   Certain short sentences are heard repeatedly during courtroom testimony (for example: *is that right, isn't that right, is that correct, isn't that true, do you know, do you recall*). These should be preceded by a semicolon.

Correct

> He paid you $25 an hour; is that correct?
> You didn't see the auto beforehand; is that right?
> There's some doubt about her identity; can you recall her?
> Was he present at that meeting; do you recall?
> You last saw Patty Raye on June 6th of this year; isn't that true?

Wrong

> You last saw Patty Raye on June 7th of this year, isn't that true?

273   The CR must distinguish between true compound sentences and those that use "echo questions." An echo question occurs at the end of a sentence and is usually, though not necessarily, negative. Never use a semicolon before an echo question.

Correct

He wouldn't tell you, would he?
Harmon is your former husband, isn't he?
You did not give him the correct information, did you?
You could see the park from your room, couldn't you?

Wrong

You could see that park from your room; couldn't you?

If distinguishing between sentences with echo questions and "regular" compound sentences is confusing, think about the difference between the following:

He was your supervisor; is that correct?
He was your supervisor, wasn't he?

The pause in the first sentence is more defined than the pause at the same point in the second version. The length of a pause is certainly not always a valid test for punctuation, but it may serve well here for identifying echos.

274 The CR must be aware of exactly what a question like "is that correct?" refers to. On occasion, another sentence may be inserted between the two.

Miss Timms left the company in 1980. That was six years ago. Is that correct?

In this case, the question refers not to the second sentence, but to the first one. The questioner is not asking if "six years ago" is a correct calculation. A period should be used, not a semicolon, because of the intervening sentence.

There was no one in the theatre at the time of the killing. Your alibi is rock solid. Isn't that true?

275 Traditional grammar would not allow a semicolon after a question. However, this is sometimes acceptable for the CR in certain constructions, complying with the requirement of asking one question at a time.

How did you get to work that day; do you remember?
Can you identify the woman; is that she?
When did you become a U.S. citizen; was it this year?

276 When an independent clause appears midsentence, do not use semicolons; instead, treat it as a parenthetical element and set it off with commas or dashes.

Afterward you went straight home, isn't that correct, and
   you did not see a doctor until the next week.
You were willing to go along with Sophia's plan—you told
   us that yourself—until you met with her accomplice.

277   A semicolon is the preferred punctuation before a conjunctive adverb
           (*however, indeed, moreover, thus, nonetheless,* etc.) that separates two inde-
           pendent clauses.

Correct

We suspected that he was dishonest; nonetheless, we tried
   to give him a fair chance.

Acceptable

We suspected that he was dishonest. Nonetheless, we tried
   to give him a fair chance.

Wrong

We suspected that he was dishonest, nonetheless, we tried
   to give him a fair chance.

Preferred

Mary wasn't receptive to the new idea; indeed, she rejected
   it entirely.
He tried to tell her of the danger; however, she turned a
   deaf ear.
It was plainly a case of theft; nevertheless, the police officer
   ignored it.

278   Use a semicolon before a transitional phrase (*on the other hand, for exam-
           ple, in fact, in other words,* etc.) that occurs between two independent
           clauses. A transitional phrase has exactly the same function as a con-
           junctive adverb.

Correct

We knew some money was missing; in fact, he was missing
   about $200.

Acceptable

We knew some money was missing. In fact, he was missing about $200.

Wrong

We knew some money was missing, in fact, he was missing
   about $200.

Preferred

There was the suggestion of mystery about the ruined palace; on the other hand, I was overimaginative in those days.

The road was narrow there; however, the other route was unpaved.

He is a true professional; in fact, he has been commended by several associations.

Note: A period can be used in place of the semicolon before conjunctive adverbs and transitional phrases, but this is considered less desirable than the semicolon *unless* the sentence is quite long and needs to be broken up.

The task was overwhelming in its complexity, and it will doubtless require endless diligence, effort, research, and literally hundreds of hours of work. On the other hand, nothing worthwhile comes easily, or so it is said.

279 Deciding what punctuation mark to use before an expression like *that is, for example,* or *namely* can be troublesome. The applicable rule is this: If what follows is a complete sentence, use a semicolon; for very long constructions, use a period; if what follows is not a complete sentence, use a comma.

Correct

The student was moving very slowly, that is, slower than the rest of the class.

BUT: The student was moving very slowly; that is, he was slower than the rest of the class.

Correct

We have found only one problem with this company, namely, its lack of fringe benefits.

BUT: We have found only one problem with this company; namely, there are no fringe benefits.

Correct

I recommended that the child read some of the classics, for example, "Treasure Island."

BUT: I recommended that the child read some of the classics; for example, "Treasure Island" is a good choice.

Wrong

I recommended that the child read some of the classics, for
example, "Treasure Island" is a good choice.

280   Three or more closely related sentences may be joined by semicolons,
although such use should be limited to situations where the sentences
are relatively short and closely associated in thought.

We invited Mary; Joe, her brother, came, too; Billy was
unavailable.
The water was cold; we were accustomed to moderate tem-
peratures; we swam for less than an hour.

Note: If the clauses are quite short and flow smoothly, commas can
be used. Again, the CR should be careful in using such a
construction.

Jim came home, he turned on the radio, he lay down on
the sofa.
I came, I saw, I conquered.

281   Use a semicolon to separate long subordinate clauses that begin with
the word *that*. This is a common occurrence in legal language.

We intend to prove today that the defendant did willfully
and intentionally lie under oath; that he did knowingly
and maliciously plan and intend to take from the property of Mrs. Williams, his employer, her jewelry and
cash; that he, the defendant, did abuse the trust Mrs.
Williams had placed in him as a trusted employee; and
that the defendant is guilty of all charges listed in the
indictment.

282   The semicolon is used to separate two independent clauses that are
joined by a coordinating conjunction (that is, in a compound sentence)
if one or both of the clauses contain commas.

When the arbiters arrived, negotiations had stopped, silence was the order of the day, and nothing was being
accomplished; but within six hours talks had resumed.
She ran up to her brother, slapped him across the face,
shouted, and began to weep; and then he grabbed her
tightly around the shoulders.
You may decide to tell us the whole story, all details included, nothing omitted; or you may decide to tell us
only what you think is relevant to this situation.

He may not rejoin this institution within a period of two years unless, of course, a pardon is issued by the chairman, the president, or the superintendent; nor will he be able to join any of the sister institutions within this state.

283   Use semicolons to separate elements of a series when the elements themselves contain commas.

The impounded automobiles include a Renault, a French car; two Saabs, Swedish cars; a Jaguar, British; and five Chevrolets.

My former addresses include 23 Yearling Lane, Raleigh, North Carolina; 557-3 Meadow Avenue, Savannah, Georgia; and 1141-4 West End Avenue, New York, New York.

The officers attending the meeting included the president, Tom Mendez; the acting chairman of finance, Carla Parkin; the regional manager, Ellen Immo; and the firm's chief accountant, Jeffrey Unger.

284   Use semicolons to separate references containing commas.

I plan to quote from Title IV, Section 8; Title V, Section 2, paragraph 20; Title VIII, Section 1, paragraph 4.

285   Use a semicolon with long enumerations, but not with short lists.

The plan is to (1) consult with experts in the field who would be able to give us some idea of the market; (2) conduct a formal, wide-range market search; (3) prepare advertisements and solicit new business; (4) go into the project full-force when the market appears ready for us.

BUT: You may (1) sign the check, (2) return it unsigned, or (3) negotiate further.

286   Remember that a semicolon is always placed outside quotation marks. When a quotation ends with a semicolon, the semicolon should be omitted entirely.

He said, "Our victory is inevitable"; however, I do not share his confidence.

She said to him, "You don't know what's going on here"; in fact, he hadn't even been home in two years.

Exercise

Correct any errors involving colons and semicolons in the following sentences. Some sentences are correct.

1. My son and my two daughters: They are my primary concern.

2. Our marriage was plagued by one problem, money.

3. Mr. Eaton left for France; isn't that true, but you were unable to go along with him.

4. Carlton Manning: what is your profession and with what firm are you employed?

5. You wouldn't deceive me; would you?

6. Luci is a clever girl; indeed, she is the most talented student I have ever taught.

7. There is only one issue now, did you steal the money?

8. Maria walked over to Louis, and did she say the following to him:

9. Sheila put three things in her purse, namely, her wallet, a revolver, and a set of keys.

10. We argued often about Freda's problems: for instance, her tantrums.

11. She instructed her children to stay off the phone, thus, they told their friends to drop by rather than telephone.

12. The following persons are to see me this afternoon. Bring pencil and paper: Jill Conrad, Alicia Grant, Boris Abbott, and David Perrine.

13. He made only this one demand, $15,000 in cash by Friday.

14. Our best secretary was: Miss Twombley.

15. Only two courses were available at that time: sociology and chemistry.

16. How often did he come around, do you remember?

17. He didn't drink before driving that night, did he?

18. Terese purchased four items: paper, pen, dictionary, and a stapler from my shop, and then she went home.

19. We were concerned about Dad's health, in fact, we were frantic.

20. Study the following passages: Section 34, page 185, paragraph 4, Section 71, page 288, paragraph 2, Section 125, page 419, paragraph 6.

The Dash

The CR's use of the dash should be limited primarily to indicating either a shift in thought or an interruption of some kind. Other uses of the dash acceptable in traditional grammar are considered a poor punctuation choice for the CR or are not permitted at all. Overuse of the dash would indicate, at times inaccurately, hesitancy on the speaker's part. Dashes should not be inserted each time a speaker falters, hesitates, pauses, or slows down. Use the dash discriminately and only when it is the decidedly best choice. The dash should be used with special care when punctuating the words of a judge or attorney.

There are certain situations in which accurate reporting demands use of the dash. It is the CR's task to be alert to these situations and to produce a transcript which, through use of the dash, will more clearly reveal to any reader exactly what transpired during the proceedings. The dash is a useful tool for preventing misreading in many circumstances.

287   The dash is used to indicate interruption of the speaker by another person. Meanings can be altered by the incorrect use or omission of the dash, and the CR must record interruptions meticulously. Do not use the ellipsis to indicate interruption.

Q. Will you cooperate with this investigation?
A. I will—
Q. Just answer yes or no, Mr. Juarez.
A. I will not be part of this fiasco. No.

> **Note:** If the CR had used a period after *I will*, the transcript would not make any sense. First the witness would be saying that he would cooperate, and then he would be saying he would not. The dash, then, is an essential element in understanding the proceedings.

288   When a speaker is interrupted and then resumes what he or she was saying after the interruption, use a pair of dashes.

Q. Did you discuss this problem with Jim Langley?
A. I discussed only—
Q. Speak up, Miss Adams.
A. —that I had discovered a problem in his bookkeeping.

The resumption does not begin with a capital letter unless it is a proper noun or the pronoun *I*.

Q. Did you see the—
A. When do you mean?

Q. Right after the fire.
A. Okay.
Q. —the man the police call David M. Smith?
A. Yes, I saw him.
Q. Can you describe the incident—

Mr. Jensen: Your question is entirely too vague.
Ms. Davids: It relied upon the preceding body of questions.
Mr. Jensen: I regard it as vague; why don't you be specific?

Q. (By Ms. Davids): —that occurred on the 15th of last month at approximately 6:30 p.m.?
A. I recall it.

289 When a speaker is interrupted by a person who then continues and completes what the speaker was saying, a pair of dashes is used.

Q. Furthermore, all the accountants in the firm—
A. —had access to the documents? Yes, they all did. But we were all told by our supervisor that we were—
Q. —immune from prosecution?
A. Yes, that's right.

290 Shifts in thought pattern are indicated with dashes.

Q. Where was Sheila at that time?
A. She was—I'm wondering what she has to do with this.

Q. How do you know that?
A. I saw in the files—are you doubting my word?

291 Noticeable hesitancy or doubt is recorded by using a pair of dashes if the hesitancy is bypassed and the sentence resumed, by a single dash if not resumed.

Q. What did the defendant say to you?
A. He said—I think I heard him say—for me to leave.

Q. What was Terrence's relationship to Mr. Barre?
A. He was his—I think, at least, but I'm not sure—his nephew.

The pilot—I'm not sure if it was the pilot or the co-pilot.

292 An abrupt shift is recorded with a dash or a pair of dashes.

Q. Did you hear anything?
A. I was humming—no, I was singing—loudly and couldn't hear a thing other than my own voice.

293   If the speaker suddenly thinks of something else he or she wishes to say, in the middle of a sentence, the dash is used to indicate this phenomenon.

Q. When did you first hear the news?
A. Mrs. Bradley telephoned me at about nine o'clock—she's 85 years old—to tell me about it.

Q. How long did you own the property?
A. I owned it from 1961 until last year—that whole area was virtually unpopulated—when I sold it to Mr. Rocca.

294   If the speaker realizes abruptly that he or she has made an assumption that should not have been made and subsequently expresses that realization, a dash is placed at that point.

Q. When you purchased the equipment from Mr. Yargar—you did purchase the equipment from Mr. Yargar?
A. I did, yes.

Q. Where did you find the diary, Miss Armstrong?
A. I found it in the library—you mean Mary Thornton's diary?

295   Sometimes the speaker will have a sudden recollection; this should be indicated by a dash.

Q. Was he wearing a hat?
A. I don't know if—he did have a hat on.

Q. Why did your mother wish to see Martin?
A. I have no idea why she—oh, it was about her will.

Note: In the first example above, note that the omission of the dash would present the reader with the exact opposite meaning. Look at the difference between the two versions, with and without the dash.

I don't know if—he did have a hat on.
I don't know if he did have a hat on.

The first sentence makes it clear that the speaker has recalled that the man was wearing a hat, but the second version would indicate that the speaker does not know whether he was wearing one.

296   When a parenthetical statement is used, the CR should insert a dash both before and after the parenthetical. The speaker has thought of something in the middle of the sentence, makes the statement, and then resumes with the original statement. Parentheticals may contain internal punctuation, which is applied just as it would be if the parenthetical were an independent statement.

I told you—I have several witnesses, you know—that I was
at the theatre all night.

Mr. Dunning was president—I worked for him for 22
years—and I was his executive assistant for the last 16
years of that time.

For parentheticals that represent a less distinct break, a comma can
be used in place of each dash, although a dash is usually acceptable.

He was my friend, and he never doubted my loyalty, for
30 years.

297   Explanatory words that occur in the middle of a sentence can be set
off with dashes.

The notion of DNA transfer—DNA being genetic
blueprints—was not accepted until recently.

Several of my best students—for example, Susan Millmann,
Cary Tanner, and Raymond Frann—have applied for a
scholarship.

The plan he suggested—the most absurd I ever heard—will
not be approved.

298   Some situations that would seem to call for a colon must use a pair
of dashes instead because the sentence continues after the "listing."

Give me the details—time, place, persons—involved in the
confrontation.

BUT: Give me the details: time, place, persons.

299   Explanatory words that occur at the end of a sentence may be preceded
by a dash, although in most cases a comma would serve equally well.

I thought he was tired—tired to the point of exhaustion.

I thought he was tired, tired to the point of exhaustion.

He was a faithful public servant—a bureaucrat in every
sense of the word.

He was a faithful public servant, a bureaucrat in every
sense of the word.

We saw several dignitaries there—the mayor, Senator Hall,
and Dennis Fallwinn.

Note: In the last example above, the dash is a better choice than
the comma, although a colon could have been used.

BUT: We saw several dignitaries there—the mayor, Senator Hall, and Dennis Fallwinn, all of whom were supporting the project.

In the above example, the dash is the only effective punctuation. A colon could not be used, and a comma would be too weak to effectively separate the "list" from the rest of the sentence because the list itself contains commas.

300   In certain situations, appositives are best set off with dashes. Appositives that contain commas should be set off with dashes.

There were four high schools—Westfield, Tyrone, O'Hara, and Davis—that attended the conference at the state capitol building.
Helen was an accomplished woman—a pianist, equestrienne, writer, and teacher—although never recognized as such by her family.

Serious ambiguity can result unless appositives that occur within a series are correctly punctuated.

Mother, Father, my teacher—Mr. Shaw, Uncle Jim, Sally Li, and Beryl met me that night at Les Fleurs Restaurant.

Note: If *Mr. Shaw* were set off by commas, the sentence would read differently: Mr. Shaw and the teacher would seem to be two individuals rather than the same person. The same principle applies to the following example.

The United States, the U.S.S.R., France, Japan—the host nation, Korea, and Belgium sent representatives.

At the beginning of a sentence, an appositive that consists of a series can be followed by a dash. A colon is an alternate punctuation. The same applies to appositives at the end of a sentence.

Jim, Marcus, and Terry—those boys were with me in my car when the accident happened.
Constancy, diligence, and strength—such attributes are admirable.
We traveled through several states—Maryland, Virginia, West Virginia, Tennessee, and Georgia.

301   Do not use a dash between two closely related sentences. Whereas this practice is sometimes acceptable in other disciplines, it is unacceptable for the CR's purposes.

Correct

Betty Morris is an excellent speaker; she will speak at our convention.

Avoid

Betty Morris is an excellent speaker—she will speak at our annual convention.

302 Do not use dashes to indicate a speaker's slowness, stuttering, or any speech pattern. Dashes would be distracting and unnecessary.

Avoid

I have—not—seen him—in two years.

Correct

I have not seen him in two years.

It is not the CR's job to record accents, dialects, or speech impediments. Learn to distinguish between speech patterns and interruptions or shifts that are essential to the meaning of what was spoken.

303 Do not use dashes for the attorneys' or judge's words unless absolutely necessary, that is, when no other mark can do the job.

304 Be conservative with the use of the dash. A transcript peppered with dashes is visually distracting. Do not use it without a concrete reason and a conviction that it will clarify the transcript's meaning.

The Comma

Proper use of the comma seems to present one of the greatest points of confusion for the CR (and for many other people, too!). Placing commas where they do not belong and omitting them where they do belong are common errors. Correct comma use requires a thorough knowledge of grammar, including an ability to recognize the difference between phrases and clauses and the difference between independent and dependent clauses. A misplaced comma can change the meaning of what was said and confuse the reader.

A common misuse of the comma in transcripts is inserting a comma to indicate a speaker's pauses or hesitations. This widespread practice produces a manuscript that is distorted and, ultimately, incorrect in its representation of what occurred and what was said. Whereas many commas do reflect natural pauses, the CR must not attempt to punctuate transcripts on that basis alone.

The three primary uses of the comma are (1) to separate, (2) to introduce, and (3) to enclose. The CR should use a comma only when a sound reason for its use can be given; otherwise, omit the comma.

305   A comma is used to separate independent clauses connected by a coordinating conjunction.

Correct

The defendant has stated that she was in Ohio then, but Mr. Gaines saw her in San Francisco on August 15th.

Note: The comma is placed before, not after, the conjunction.

We rode down to Springville, and we spent the day there with Aunt Mae.

Wrong

We rode down to Springville and, we spent the day there with Aunt Mae.

306   If there is no conjunction between two independent clauses, a comma cannot and must not be used to separate the clauses. A period or semicolon should be used in this place.

Correct

Your testimony is that you were at work on June 7, 1984, from 9:00 until 5:00; you state that you did not leave the office until 5:00, not even for lunch.

Wrong

Your testimony is that you were at work on June 7, 1984, from 9:00 until 5:00, you state that you did not leave the office until 5:00, not even for lunch.

Correct

I asked him to accompany me. He refused to go unless I paid his fare.

Acceptable

I asked him to accompany me; he refused to go unless I paid his fare.

Wrong

I asked him to accompany me, he refused to go unless I paid his fare.

307   If two independent clauses connected by a coordinating conjunction are very short, or the first one is very short, the comma is optional. The comma can be omitted when there is no possibility of confusing or misleading the reader.

> I was afraid and I said so.
> Jimmy left the room and Marcia ran after him.

308   Three or more independent clauses can be joined by commas.

> We will go to Monroe Bank to apply for a loan, or you
> may wish to consider asking your brother for the
> money, or perhaps George can sell his car to get cash.
> We worked on the house all day, we stopped at around six
> o'clock, and we all had dinner out at Sam's.

309   If two independent clauses are connected by a conjunction and either or both clauses contain commas, a semicolon can replace the comma that separates the clauses. This is a judgment left to the CR and usually is not necessary if only one comma is used within either clause.

> Yes, we have seen the samples, but we simply are not
> interested in buying at this time.
> It is, in my humble opinion, not desirable to have Joseph
> testify; but, in Mr. Grant's opinion, we will have to do
> it sooner or later anyway.
> The red, the white, and the yellow shirts are clean; but
> you may wish to launder, iron, and hang them to be
> sure they are fresh for Mr. Burns, who is a particular
> man when it comes to his wardrobe.

310   At times witnesses or attorneys will engage in what seem to be endless sentences that ramble on forever. It is acceptable for the conscientious CR to separate these long constructions with periods and semicolons. In fact, it is more than merely acceptable; it is highly desirable, for clarity's sake, to cut up excessively long constructions into shorter ones.

The following is an example of such a rambling passage:

> Bring your records of all transactions during the past five
> years, and be prepared to open these records, but be certain
> that you have brought everything available and have omitted
> nothing, but if elements are missing, Mr. Daniels, you must
> be prepared to explain, if possible, such omissions, and you can
> be sure that you will be questioned thoroughly.

A CR could punctuate the passage more effectively by replacing some of the commas with semicolons and/or periods.

> Bring your records of all transactions during the past five years, and be prepared to open these records; but be certain that you have brought everything available and have omitted nothing. But if elements are missing, Mr. Daniels, you must be prepared to explain, if possible, such omissions; and you can be sure that you will be questioned thoroughly.

The following example also started as one long sentence containing independent clauses joined by coordinating conjunctions. It has been cut up into smaller sentences by using periods and semicolons rather than commas between some of these clauses.

> I thought that he was going to return after a couple of hours; so I told Mr. Ellis to wait for him there, and he told me that he would wait. And then I just let Mr. Ellis sit down in the waiting room, but I didn't watch what he was doing or anything like that, for it hadn't occurred to me that I needed to keep an eye on him, and I knew that Ed Johnson knew him. But I did walk into the waiting room several times to get this or that, and I didn't notice him doing anything except looking through magazines; and once he was looking out the window, sort of staring out as though he was worried. But I didn't want to disturb him, you know.

311   Commas separate items in a series. The items separated can be words, phrases, or clauses. A series consists of more than two items. The "serial" comma, that is, the final comma before the conjunction, should be used, despite a somewhat wide tendency to omit this final comma. The only situation in which the serial comma should be omitted is when the two final items are a unit rather than individual items.

> I then gathered my case, keys, wallet, and hat.
> She needs to type a confirmation letter, a memorandum of record, and a mailing list.
> The breakfast specials were blueberry pancakes, oatmeal, and ham and eggs.

> **Note:** There is no comma after *ham* because *ham and eggs* is a unit.

> We looked for the missing cat under the bed, behind the sofa, and on the armchair.
> Wading in the river, lunching on the grounds, hiking through the woods, and playing games in the field gave the kids a wonderful holiday.

He hoped to graduate from college, to travel for a full year, to keep a travel journal, and then to return home.

We worked all day, we went home at dusk, and we listened to music until time to retire.

Whenever he saw his former wife, whenever he ran out of money, and whenever he had difficulty with his staff—these were times when his mood darkened.

You should have informed us where you would arrive, when you would be there, where I could reach you, and how you planned to spend the evening.

Mrs. Bates asked for you, Mr. Kelvin telephoned, Ms. Demper came by, and Mrs. James left several messages.

312   Omit the comma when the conjunction is repeated in a series.

The woman shouted and cried and pleaded with the two men.

BUT: The woman shouted, cried, and pleaded with the two men.

We drove around the mountain range and into the valley and through the town of Millerville.

BUT: We drove around the mountain range, into the valley, and through the town of Millerville.

313   For clauses in a series, if the conjunction is repeated and the clauses are independent, retain the commas.

I boarded the train at noon as planned, and I noticed the man as one I'd seen before, but I couldn't recall from where.

We drove until dark, and then we stopped in Kansas City, but we left there before dawn the next morning.

314   Do not use commas if dependent clauses are connected by conjunctions.

Before you call Mary and before you do anything about Harriet's problem and when you know the situation, then you can call my brother.

BUT: Before you call Mary, before you do anything about Harriet's problem, when you know the situation, then you can call my brother.

If he calls me and if I feel like going and if you don't mind being alone, I'll go to the concert.

But: If he calls me, if I feel like going, if you don't mind being alone, I'll go to the concert.

315   If the elements in a series contain commas with the elements themselves, the commas should be replaced by semicolons. This is to make the separation between the elements clear.

Correct

We planned to stop in Baltimore, Maryland; Washington, D.C.; New York, New York; Boston, Massachusetts; and Newport, Rhode Island.

Wrong

We planned to stop in Baltimore, Maryland, Washington, D.C., New York, New York, Boston, Massachusetts, and Newport, Rhode Island.

Note: Using a semicolon rather than a comma in such situations is not only desirable but frequently necessary to the meaning of the sentence. In the example that follows, the sentence can be misread to be a list of almost twice as many people as it really includes, a situation clarified by the use of the semicolon.

Members present at the board meeting included Mr. Jaffe, the president of the club, Miss Wallis, the organization's secretary, Tom Carr, the chairman, and Noel Richards.

It is far clearer to use semicolons, and misreading is thus prevented:

Members present at the board meeting included Mr. Jaffe, the president of the club; Miss Wallis, the organization's secretary; Tom Carr, the chairman; and Noel Richards.

316   Adjectives in a series that modify the same word or group of words are separated by commas.

The children saw a growling, vicious, snarling dog standing before them, and there was fear in their pale, wide-eyed faces.

Dorrell carried a small brown puppy in her arms.

Why are there commas separating the adjectives in the first sentence but not those in the second sentence? This issue is complex and difficult to master. The comma is placed between adjectives that modify the *same* noun to the same *degree*. The word *small* modifies the term *brown puppy*, not just *puppy*. There are a couple of "tests" that work well in deciding whether to place commas between adjectives. The CR can use one or the other of these tests—or both—to help in deciding whether or not commas should be used.

Test #1

If the word *and* can be inserted logically between the adjectives, then a comma is used. For example, one would not say "the small and brown puppy" but instead "the small brown puppy." The *and* does not logically fit; therefore, no comma is used. However, one could say "the growling and vicious and snarling dog" and still sound correct; thus the comma should be used.

> The angelic little children sang a song to cheer her.
> The sunny, warm weather inspired us to do something
>   outdoors.

> APPLYING TEST #1:

> You would *not* say "angelic and little children."
> You *would* say "sunny and warm weather."

Test #2

If the order of the adjectives is reversed, is the original meaning retained and does the reversed order sound "right"? If so, use a comma between the adjectives; if not, use no comma.

> The enormous white mansion on the hill belongs to
>   Mr. Pibb.

> APPLYING TEST #2:

> The white enormous mansion on the hill belongs to
>   Mr. Pibb.

Reversing the order does not work well; therefore, no comma should separate the adjectives.

> Her expensive, elegant dress is an original design.

> APPLYING TEST #2:

> Her elegant, expensive dress is an original design.

Reversing the order of the adjectives seems to work just as well as the original order; therefore, the comma is correct.

Correct

> His mocking, sneering smile angered me.
> Her thick auburn hair is her greatest asset.

The plush velvet sofa invited me to rest.

Mr. Heinrich's long, involved, thorough analysis was lying on the desk for a month before it was read.

317   Never use a comma before a series begins.

Correct

He implied that we were lonely, neurotic, and depressed.

Wrong

He implied that we were, lonely, neurotic, and depressed.

318   Short introductory phrases (usually four or fewer words) often do not require a comma. Phrases of five words or more should be followed by a comma. Sometimes even very short phrases must be followed by a comma to avoid confusion.

During the proceedings she wept silently.
During the first several days of testimony, she wept silently.
In 1981 we were living in Utah with our sister and her husband.
In order to complete the picture of that night's events, we will need to have you tell your story once again.
Under the bed, linens were stacked up and gathering dust.

Note: In the last example, the comma separating *bed* and *linens* makes the sentence easier to read. Without the comma *bed linens* may be incorrectly read as a single entity.

After his arrival we sat down to talk.
After his arrival at our house, we sat down to talk.

319   Mild interjections are followed by a comma, whereas strong interjections are followed by an exclamation point. This is a judgment call for the CR that will be indicated by voice tone, emotion or lack of it, and expressions.

Oh, I don't know how she got there.
You fool! Don't ask me that again!
Shucks, people always tell me that.

320   Introductory verbal phrases (infinitive or participial) should be followed by a comma.

To accomplish your goals, you must be diligent.
Singing merrily, Joan cleaned the entire house.

Note: Be sure to distinguish between introductory verbal phrases and verbals that serve as the subject of the sentence. There is no comma after verbals that are the subject.

> To cut down on expenses is what I was trying to do. (subject)
> To cut down on expenses, I cook my own meals now. (introductory infinitive phrase)
> Purchasing a home was a big step for us. (subject)
> Purchasing a home together, the couple had taken a big step. (introductory participial phrase)

321 Direct address at the beginning of a sentence should be followed by a comma. In the middle of a sentence, it should be set off with commas, and at the end of a sentence it is preceded by a comma.

> Have a seat, Mr. Wilkins.
> Mr. Wilkins, have a seat.
> Where, John Wilkins, would you like to sit?

322 Commas are sometimes necessary to avoid possible misreading or slowing down of the reading.

> Outside, the yard was becoming soggy and muddy.

Note: If the comma is omitted after *outside*, the reader will at first see it as the beginning of the prepositional phrase *outside the yard*.

> Before cleaning, the child made her ritual complaints about doing chores.

Note: Again, the comma after *cleaning* prevents the misreading *before cleaning the child*.

323 Use a comma after introductory words (*well, yes, no, however, nevertheless, briefly, actually, similarly, unfortunately, nevertheless*).

> Yes, I understand the question.
> Actually, we were not aware of his exploits until recently.
> Unfortunately, the meeting had to be cancelled.
> Indeed, we have several objections.

Sometimes careful inspection is necessary. What may appear at first glance to be an introductory word may perform another function in the sentence. Look at the following examples:

> Now I understand what you mean.

> BUT: Now, I can see your side of the problem, but it's not my place to sympathize.

In the first sentence, *now* is an adverb; in the second, it is an introductory word. Examine the following sentences.

> However I try, he will not cooperate with me.
> However, he will not cooperate with me.
> Well, I like to drink water with my meals.
> Well water tastes odd to me.

324   Do not use a comma after a coordinating conjunction that begins a sentence.

Correct

> And we have the truth at last.
> But are you certain?

Wrong

> And, we have the truth at last.
> But, are you certain?

325   Sometimes a comma is appropriate after *yes* or *no*; in other situations a period is the appropriate mark. This is determined by the content of the sentence. If *yes* or *no* is answering a question but supplying no other information whatsoever, a comma is used. If the answer goes on to supply additional information, use a period.

Q. Is Jason sick?
A. Yes, he is.

BUT:

Q. Is Jason sick?
A. Yes. He has been sick for two weeks, and he has not improved at all.

Q. Have you lived at that house for more than a year?
A. No, sir, I have not.

BUT:

Q. Have you lived at that house for more than a year?
A. No, sir. I have been living there only two months—since July.

326   Use a comma to separate a statement from an echo question that follows. (See the section on semicolons in this unit.)

> You were on your way home, weren't you?
> You could hear what they were saying, couldn't you?
> You wouldn't betray me, would you?

BUT:

You were present when Eli attacked Willis; is that correct?
Mr. Chira gave you the money; isn't that true?

327   Commas usually set off appositives.

William Randall, my attorney, should be present when you
speak with me.
Daria Towley, the girl who won the scholarship, has
disappeared.
The best plan, or at least the one our president selects, will
be implemented immediately.
All of my students, especially Carl Marrow, have improved
this semester.
The most charming man I have ever met, Ben Petersen, is
also the most outrageous scoundrel.

- Remember that titles, academic degrees, and abbreviations after a
name, such as *Jr.*, *Sr.*, *Esquire*, *Inc.*, and *Limited*, are appositive in
nature and should be set off with commas.

Mr. John Lester, Jr., has won an award that will bring
him new recognition.
Litton and Bridges, Inc., has won the contract.
Ralph Martin, Ph.D., will teach the course.

EXCEPTION: Roman numerals after a name.

George Morrison Zale III is my father.

- Do not set off an appositive that is part of a title.

Alexander the Great is remembered in several plays.
William the Conqueror is the subject of his study.

- Use quotation marks, not commas, to set off a word, phrase, expression, etc., used as an appositive.

The term "indisputable" is not appropriate.
We were told that the phrase "in reply to your letter"
is trite and should not be used in company correspondence.

- Set off identifying or explanatory phrases that begin with *of*.

Mr. Henry Zeller, of our Chicago office, is preparing a
report.
Miss Jane Dunmore, of British Columbia and London,
was visiting her aunt in New York City.

- If an appositive is restrictive in nature, it should not be set off by commas. This is an area of confusion for many and often requires extra thought.

> Of my three sons, my son Jeremy has the best sense of humor. (restrictive because it distinguishes which one of the three sons)
> Tracy's only son, Christopher, is seriously ill. (nonrestrictive because there is only one son)
> Betty Smith's novel "A Tree Grows in Brooklyn" was one of my favorites when I was in high school. (restrictive because she wrote more than one novel)
> His one novel, "Terror in the Attic," was a dismal failure.
> The year 1979 was a trouble-filled time for my family.
> The best year of my life, 1981, was when we traveled through Europe.

328   Set off each item in a date.

> On December 2, 1983, we were married in Denver.

> EXCEPTION: When using only the month and year, or when writing the date in inverted style (2 December 1983), the comma is unnecessary.

> During June 1979 she suffered a heart seizure of some kind.
> I first met Mel on 18 March 1980.

329   A comma is used before a short quotation.

> Dr. Baker said, "I cannot find any broken bones in your foot."
> Melinda asked, "Why are you here?"

330   Set off the word *please* when it occurs at the end of a sentence and sometimes in the middle of a sentence.

> Let us come in for a few moments, please.
> Tell us, please, where you were when she died.

> BUT: Will you please tell us where you were when she died.

331   Set off *etc.* within a sentence.

> Transcripts, contracts, exhibits, etc., were placed in a safe.

332 When city and state are written together, commas are placed after both.

> Columbus, Ohio, is the site of the new factory.
> We were planning a national conference in New Orleans, Louisiana, that would last for an entire week.

333 Adjectives that follow the word they modify should be set off by commas.

> The house, isolated and crumbling, was his only property.
> The child, frightened and alone, whimpered as she walked down the sidewalk.

334 It is usually preferable not to use a comma in a sentence that has a compound verb but is not a compound sentence.

> Fletcher watched as the boys fought but took no action to break up the fight.
>
> BUT: Fletcher watched as the boys fought, but he took no action to break up the fight. (The addition of a second subject, *he*, makes this a compound sentence.)

If the elements of the compound verb are very long, or if a contrast is being emphasized, a comma is sometimes used.

> I wasn't fighting, but rather debating.

335 Parenthetical elements are set off by commas except when dashes seem more appropriate.

> He is, I believe, president of the company.
> He was, to put it mildly, a poor sport.

336 Company names that employ an ampersand omit the comma before the ampersand.

> Hays, Milton & Sach have opened a new office on 25th Street.

337 Introductory dependent clauses usually are followed by a comma.

> Whenever we met, we argued about one thing or another.
> If you can, come to the shop tonight.
> Because he failed math, he will attend summer school.

338   Commas follow conjunctive adverbs and transitional phrases.

>We hoped he would win a scholarship; on the other hand, we had saved enough money for his college tuition if he did not win one.
>
>Kalla Marks was granted a new hearing; however, a reversal is not anticipated.
>
>He was considered a security risk; indeed, he was not allowed on the premises.

339   Elements in an address (except zip codes) are separated by commas.

>Send the package to Room 38, 75 West 88th Street, New York City 10017.
>
>His office is being moved to Room 112, Floor 5, Annex A, Bates Building.

340   Nonrestrictive elements are set off by commas.

>The employee who is honest and works hard will get ahead in this company. (restrictive)
>
>Mr. Warren, who is one of the hardest workers in this company, has just been promoted. (nonrestrictive)

In the first sentence, *who is honest and works hard* is a restrictive clause; that is, it is essential to the meaning of the sentence. Take it out and we have: *The employee will get ahead in this company.* The restrictive clause identifies exactly which employee will get ahead. In the second sentence, Mr. Warren is not identified by the clause. The nonrestrictive clause *who is one of the hardest workers in this company* gives the reader additional information about Mr. Warren, but removing it does not alter the essential meaning of the sentence.

>There are two Mr. Carls in my neighborhood, but I am acquainted only with the Mr. Carl who works for Exxon. (restrictive)
>
>Samuel Carl, who is a barber, lives near me. (nonrestrictive)
>
>The plan that you suggest cannot solve our problems. (restrictive)
>
>Plan C, which is the best we have seen, will be adopted. (nonrestrictive)

>**Note:** Clauses that begin with *that* are not set off by commas.

>The boy that I saw was tall and thin.
>
>One of the most beautiful places that we visited was Tokyo.

Children like Amos need special attention. (restrictive)
Our nation's largest cities, like Chicago and New York,
will be highlighted in this book. (nonrestrictive)

341   Use a comma to indicate contrast.

I went to talk, not to argue.
I expected to receive a little money, but not a fortune.

342   Use a comma to separate identical words when confusion could occur.

Come in, in a few minutes.
I warn you, you cannot refuse to cooperate with us.

343   When a numbered list occurs in a sentence, a comma follows the written-out version of the number. If what was said was "one . . . two . . . three," etc., numerals in parentheses are used; if what was said was "first . . . second . . . third," etc., these ordinals are written as words, not numbers.

I want you to tell us these things: first, when you met
Paul Matthieson; second, what he said to you;
and, third, why you kept this meeting secret from
Silvio.

Do not use commas after the numerals in numbered lists:

The package contained the following items: (1) four pamphlets, (2) three pencils, and (3) an empty envelope.

344   Use commas to set off *for example, for instance, namely,* and *that is* if what follows such a term is not a complete sentence. If what follows is a complete sentence, use a semicolon before the term and a comma after it.

We saw several of our co-workers there, namely, Richard
O'Hara, Barbara LeBlanc, Oscar Schoen, and Terrence
Vale.
He is allergic to some foods, for example, tomatoes and
strawberries, that he enjoys eating.
We took immediate, drastic action; that is, we filed suit
against the estate.

345   A comma can be used to indicate omitted words that are "understood."

Jan earned $50 doing odd jobs for Mr. Suarez; Zina, $80
working for us.

346   Use a comma in numbers over a thousand except in addresses, telephone numbers, and document designations.

> We sold 3,982 tickets to the concert.
> He lives at 11237 Boulder Lane.
> Policy No. 58473K-33 has been cancelled.

347   Sometimes commas are needed to separate numbers that occur adjacent to one another in a sentence.

> Of the 17, 14 passed the exam with a grade of 90 percent or better.
> On page 471, 35 persons are listed as missing from that area.

Exercise

Correct errors involving commas, dashes, and semicolons in the following.

Q. State your name please.

A. Eleanor Mary Albert.

Q. In respect to the house at issue here today; you had a purchase agreement with—

A. Nathan Sorrell.

Q. And was Mr. Sorrell, the sole owner of the house?

A. I thought he was but, I learned later that his sister, was co-owner.

Q. What is Mr. Sorrell's sister's name Miss Albert?

A. Her name is, Lianne Sorrell Reed.

Q. And, is Reed her married name?

A. Yes. It is.

Q. When did you learn that Mrs. Reed was co-owner of the house, from whom did you learn this?

A. I found out, when Mrs. Reed showed up at my door, she told me herself. Mr. Sorrell never told me, anything about it.

Q. What did she?

A. I was shocked.

Q. say to you that day?

A. She told me that I would have to move out of the house; and that I would have to move out.

Q. Did she tell you why?

A. Well she was talking fast, and acting nervous. She walked, into my house—she didn't even tell me who she was—and just started telling me how I would have to move out of the house—because the sale was not going to take place.

Q. Was this the first time you met Mrs. Reed?

A. Yes. It was actually the first time I even knew that she existed.

Q. What was your response to her, to Mrs. Reed's statements.

A. I asked her, who she was.

Q. What did she say?

A. She said—"I am the owner of this house; and I am not going to sell it to you."

Q. Is that all she said?

A. No, she told me that it had all been a big misunderstanding, but she would give me two weeks, to get out of the house.

Q. And, what was your response?

A. I told her that I had a purchase agreement with her brother Nathan Sorrell to buy the house.

Q. What was the asking price of the house, do you recall?

A. It was, I think $125,000.

Q. But the offer you made was lower than that; wasn't it?

A. Yes, I made an offer of $107,500.

Q. Did Mr. Sorrell accept—

A. Yes, he accepted my offer.

Q. Was your offer accompanied by any money?

A. Oh yes. I gave him a check for $1000—a token of good faith.

Q. Did Mr. Sorrell cash the check, or not?

A. He did cash it, yes.

Q. Tell me, Miss Albert was anyone living in the house at the time you made the offer?

A. No. It was vacant at that time and it had been vacant for several months.

Q. Miss Albert—when did you move into the house?

A. If my memory serves me well it was on June 5th.

Q. You moved into the house on June 5th; is that correct?

A. Yes, that's right.

Q. But the act of sale had not taken place yet?

A. No. It hadn't.

Q. How then were you able, to move into the house?

A. Mr. Sorrell and I had an agreement, I would go ahead and move in, and I would pay rent, until the act of sale passed.

Q. How much was it, I mean how much rent did you pay him, each month?

A. I was paying $900 each month, however, that included utilities.

Q. While you were paying this rent you still did not know that Mrs. Reed owned a half-share of the house; is that true?

A. I didn't know, how could I?

Q. You made an offer, it was accepted, and you moved into the house, right?

4

Capitalization

Rules for capitalization vary with the occupational setting. The following guidelines are tailored to the CR and will not, therefore, always coincide with those of other professions, although most will. Some sections of depositions are capitalized for reasons of tradition within the industry. In such situations the CR should follow the precedent or the preferred format of the firm for whom he or she works.

Nonetheless, there are a number of basic guidelines that a CR should use when in doubt and when the CR's firm has not specified a preference. Some of these rules are fundamental to proper English and will be uniformly observed, whereas others are specific to the CR industry. As with so many issues, the dictionary is an invaluable tool that can answer many capitalization questions that cannot be covered in a set of guidelines.

The following rules begin with general, widely observed rules and proceed to more specialized rules.

348   The first word of each new sentence and the first word of a sentence fragment should be capitalized.

Q. You say you knew what he was trying to do?
A. No way, man.
Q. Nothing at all?
A. Not an idea, not a one.

Q. Was he wearing a white jacket?
A. Hard to remember.
Q. Please try to recall.
A. All right, all right.

> **Note:** All the answers in the above examples are fragments, not complete sentences, but they all must begin with a capital letter.

349   The first word of a quotation is capitalized even when the quotation begins midsentence.

The player asked, "Do you think I'll make the team?"
He hesitated and looked at me intently before saying, "No, we sold it last week."

350   Do not capitalize the first word of the second part of a split quotation unless it should be capitalized for some other reason, e.g., a proper noun.

> "The U.S. Treasury," the Secretary asserted, "will honor all claims made by our department."
> "She repeatedly questioned me on that point," Ron mentioned, "but I told her nothing."
> "Although I expected to be awarded that recognition," Joseph lamented, "Neal Warton was the recipient instead."

351   Quoted fragments, words, or terms may or may not be capitalized, depending on their nature, but usually are not.

> His frequent feeling "under the weather" has become a problem for our company.
> That place was Miller's "Shangri-La"; I knew he went there to have his "R and R" when he was tired, anxious, or depressed.
> The newspapers referred to the "Slaughter on Elm Street" as one that could have been avoided.
> What did he mean when he called our organization "bellicose"?

352   Proper nouns are capitalized, but some of their derivatives—those that have become commonly used in everyday language—are not capitalized. Refer to your dictionary when in doubt.

> china (referring to dishes)   oriental rug
> plaster of paris   roman numerals
> scotch (the alcoholic drink)

353   Names of persons, including nicknames, are capitalized.

> She was called "Lady Edith" because of her aloof manner toward the rest of the group.
> Joseph "See All" Henry was loved by his readers.
> My friends—Josephine, Kathryn, and Marianna—were known to me and my family as Jo, Kate, and Manny.

354   Initials in names are capitalized.

> Kenneth M.J. Peoples has served the H.J. Jones Company
>   for 27 years.
> I called B.J., but there was no answer.

Note: Editorial practice varies with respect to the spacing of personal
initials. CRs should close them up as shown above.

355   Designations such as *Jr.* and *Sr.* are capitalized.

> Thomas Seigner, Jr., is my uncle as well as my boss.
> Albert Junior makes the major decisions; Albert Senior is a
>   mere figurehead.

356   Some foreign names contain elements that are not always capitalized.
This can cause confusion and should be researched by the CR, if at
all possible.

> Alphonse de la Boite is an exchange student staying with
>   my parents.
> Mr. Van Halken will arrive tomorrow night.

357   Titles are capitalized when they are accompanied by the name of the
person who possesses the title. A title used alone is not capitalized
except when it is a part of a formal list or is being used without the
name in direct address. Exceptions are the heads of states, U.S. Sena-
tors, U.S. Congressmen, and other high government officials.

> The absence of Professor Jamison has the students con-
>   cerned.

> BUT: I saw my history professor at the restaurant that
>   night.
> I refuse to vote for Senator Malia again this time; I hope
>   our Senator will be Ms. Ulane.
> Did the mayor make a brief speech, or did one of the
>   councilmen speak in his place?
> I recognized Mayor Eldon and Congressman Yuba
>   immediately.
> The ambassador was taken hostage by the terrorists.
> The President will address the press tonight.
> Can you tell us, Mayor, what the plans for that prop-
>   erty are?

358   Academic Degrees

Academic degrees and their abbreviations are capitalized when written after the name of the person having the degree. They are also capitalized when written out as a complete term. They are not capitalized when they are used in a general sense.

> I hope to have my M.S. by June.
> He has been working on his doctorate at Florida State.
> Isabel Morales, Doctor of Philosophy, will speak to our
>   group next month.
> He'll never get his medical degree, in my opinion.
> The job requires a bachelor's in sociology.

359   Nationalities and Ethnic Groups

Names of ethnic groups, nationalities, languages, and other formal groups of people are capitalized. Slang terms or terms based on "color" are not capitalized.

> The black Democratic representative said that his ques-
>   tions had been addressed satisfactorily.
> The Greek language was more difficult for me to learn
>   than was French.
> His Nordic heritage was evident in his home furnishings.
> I saw a Caucasian man and an Oriental woman enter the
>   building after midnight.

360

Names of organizations, clubs, institutions, schools, universities, commissions, committees, boards, companies, buildings, councils, and other organizations are capitalized when referring to a specific one.

> The VFW's Looking at America Committee, in associa-
>   tion with the Springfield Auxiliary Club, will meet
>   in the Springfield Municipal Building.
> The Anti-Litter Association presented its ideas to the
>   Tilton Library Council and the Board of Commu-
>   nity Improvement last night.
> Has the board of directors met this month?
> My club is looking for ideas on how to raise money.
> Isn't Ichia & Son Electric located on Ward Avenue?
> Our company had an enormous profit last year, but
>   Carlton & Missions suffered a severe loss.

361

Names of cities, counties, states, countries, continents, hemispheres, and governing bodies are capitalized when reference is made to a specific one.

The City of Jenkins and Ralph County will act together on this project.

In Louisiana counties are called parishes; my cousins live in Orleans Parish and my parents in Jefferson Parish.

While in Africa, Hans contracted a terrible fever, but I understand he's now in Europe—France, I assume.

The Western Hemisphere includes South America, you know.

362   Names of bodies of water—lakes, rivers, ponds, seas, oceans, etc.—are capitalized when reference is made to a specific body.

The Mississippi River, fed by various other rivers and streams, partially fills Lake Pontchartrain before emptying into the Gulf of Mexico.

The Sea of Denmark's ownership is hotly contested.

When James plays, he usually goes down to Miller's Stream or Lake Arrowhead, even though there are other lakes in the area.

We're digging a pond on our land; hopefully, it will be about the size of Jackoman Pond.

363   Capitalize the names of specific streets, avenues, boulevards, roads, and highways.

They now live on Hudson Boulevard, which is right off Rome Avenue; it is one of the nicest streets in this city.

Drive down Sellers Lane until you get to Highway 49 and then stay on that road for three miles.

We took U.S. Highway 2 all the way, but Interstate 91 would have been a better route.

The highway near my house is in a state of disrepair; that's why I use either the expressway or State Highway 356.

364   Names of specific bridges are capitalized.

The Golden Gate Bridge is part of an impressive landscape.

To get to Manhattan, I cross the Brooklyn Bridge or the Manhattan Bridge; I prefer either of these bridges to the tunnel.

365   The words *room* and *apartment* are capitalized when used with a number.

I'm in the same building, but I moved from Apartment 23
to No. 7.

The offices are located in Room 49 of the Tate Building,
but I don't know if they also occupy Room 52.

366   The terms *state* and *city* are capitalized when referred to in an institu-
tional or corporate sense, but not when referred to simply as a place.

The State of Wyoming will press for extradition.
I will be living in the state of Wyoming for the summer.
She lives in the city of Urbana, Illinois.
The City of Urbana is seeking government funds for the
restructuring.

367   *North, south, east, west,* and their various forms and derivatives (*north-
west, northern,* etc.) are not capitalized except when they refer to a recognized geographic area or section.

Just drive south for about six miles to find the school.
The western edge of the stadium is reserved for handi-
capped persons.
We were planning to move out West, perhaps to
California.
We couldn't persuade Marlena to leave the Northeast.
They spent most of their time at a villa in the south of
France.

368   Sections of cities or "nicknames" for areas are capitalized.

The Big Apple offers an endless variety of activities.
The South Side of Chicago is his home.
The Crescent City hosts the Mardi Gras every year.

Note: Do not use capitals except for specific nicknames or specific
geographic areas.

The south side of my street has several brownstones.
The western corner of the county is the most populated.
I was looking for an apartment in the southeast section of
town.
I found an apartment on the Upper West Side—on West
72nd Street.

A geographical dictionary can be useful in determining specific geographic areas and nicknames for cities.

369   Hyphenated words are capitalized or lowercased as they would be if
no hyphens were used.

Stratford-on-Avon is known for its native son, William
  Shakespeare.
Commander-in-Chief Richardson was out of the country
  last week.
The not-so-happy-to-be-here transfer student is making
  everyone miserable.

370   When referring to a supreme being, *God* is capitalized; when referring
to the deities of a polytheistic religion, do not capitalize. When
pronouns refer to God, they should be capitalized also.

The Greek gods were actively involved in humans' lives.
His godlike rule over his family was intolerable.
He believed that God would be his guidepost in times of
  decision.
I prayed to Him each night for guidance, but I was con-
  fused by His silence.

371   Capitalize the pronoun *I*.

He said I couldn't have my inheritance yet.
Do you think I am unaware of what was going on?

372   Capitalize the vocative *O* but not the exclamation *oh*.

The 16th-century poem read, "O Lord, have mercy on
  me."
He said—oh, I can't repeat it!

373   Diseases are not capitalized unless named for a person, generally the
one who isolated the disease. When in doubt, consult a medical
dictionary.

The diagnosis was Parkinson's disease.
Patients of the disease leprosy prefer the term Hansen's disease to describe the condition.
My grandmother, unfortunately, seems to be developing
  osteoporosis, and she also complains of slight angina and
  migraines.

374   Capitalize trade names but not generic names.

Is it true that a dapsone-resistant strain has developed?
He wanted you to purchase Headache Demolition, not
  plain aspirin.
Do you prefer Tylenol?
I take erythromycin for my throat infections.

375   Capitalize *Number* and *No.* when accompanied by the number.

> I picked No. 7 to win and No. 3 to place.
> Student I.D. Number 38721 was found on the library floor.

376   Names of political parties are capitalized; however, when the same terms are used to denote an ideology, capitals are not used.

> He expects to be the Democratic nominee for governor.
> Having you make all the decisions hardly seems democratic
>   to me!
> She thought of herself as a liberal thinker, but she was not
>   a member of the Liberal Party.
> The Whigs, once powerful, are now part of history.

377   Honors, awards, and other such forms of recognition are capitalized.

> He keeps his Purple Heart in a velvet-covered box.
> The Businessmen of the City Organization presented Mr.
>   Haney with their Mismanagement and Waste Award.
> Whom do you expect to win the Nobel Peace Prize?
> Although we have no hope of receiving the Pulitzer or the
>   National Book Award, we hope to make a nice profit.

378   Branches of the armed forces are capitalized when the full title is given.

> The U.S. Marine Corps is smaller than the U.S. Army,
>   isn't it?
> He signed up to join the marines, not the navy.
> The British air force is known as the Royal British Air
>   Force.

379   Historical events and eras are capitalized.

> The Battle of Waterloo spelled Napoleon's end.
> The Industrial Revolution shattered farm-based British life.
> I had heard that Bellam's grandmother was an eminent
>   Victorian scholar.
> The computer, although a Space Age product, has its
>   roots in the 19th century.

> **Note:** Do not capitalize the word *century* when listing centuries numerically, e.g., *20th century, fifth century.*

380   Do not capitalize *a.m.* or *p.m.*

> He was supposed to telephone me at 6:30 p.m. sharp, but
>   he did not call until after midnight.

381   Titles of books, magazines, movies, pamphlets, television and radio programs, songs, poems, and works of art are capitalized except for articles (*a, an, the*), coordinating conjunctions (*and, or, for, nor*), and prepositions of fewer than four letters, unless one of these words is the first or last word of the title or subtitle. The *to* in an infinitive is not capitalized.

> Of Faulkner's novels, "The Sound and the Fury" was the first we read.
>
> "Mysticism and Romance: A Case Study" is a bizarre account of my sister's life, but it is factual.
>
> My son was delivering "The Daily News" for about a year until he changed over to "The Weekly Chronicle" and "Shoppers' Digest" to increase his income.
>
> His best painting was "River of Tears," but it didn't sell for the high price of "Timberland" or "A Child's Joy."
>
> "Walk With Me" won several awards, including one in national competition.

382   Names designating family relationships are capitalized only when they are used as a substitute for that person's name, when they are used in direct address, or when they are used with the person's name. They are not capitalized when used with a possessive noun.

> Will the police tell Mother of Father's death, or will Uncle Ted?
>
> My brother Sam, who is out of the country right now, received a strange telephone call from someone claiming to be his uncle.
>
> Tell me something, Grandfather, about what your school was like.
>
> Come on, Cousin Jake, don't talk to your grandparents like that.
>
> My sister Ellen's hair is much darker than mine.

383   **Product Names**

The company name is capitalized, but the name of the object itself is not capitalized.

> Herb purchased a Datsun station wagon for family trips.
>
> I eat Quaker oatmeal for breakfast every morning.
>
> Alicia was saving her money to purchase an IBM typewriter.
>
> The Swingline 5000 stapling machine is the most efficient I've ever used.

384   The names of specific religions and churches are capitalized.

> Did the Anglican faith develop during the reign of Henry
> VIII?
> It would seem that Roman Catholicism meets his spiritual
> needs.
> How many Protestant churches are located in this city?
> He attends St. Paul's Episcopal Church when he is at
> home.
> The Buddhists explain reincarnation in a way that appeals
> to me.

385   The names of religious books and holidays, and of some religious
ceremonies, are capitalized.

> The King James Version of the Bible is our choice for
> study.
> His life is based on the teachings of the Koran.
> She takes Holy Communion every week.

Note: The names of most religious ceremonies are not capitalized.

> The boy's bar mitzvah could not be postponed.
> Her baptism was a special event in her religious life.

386   Do not capitalize the names of the seasons.

> We last painted our house in the spring of 1983, and we
> intend to paint it again this winter.
> We generally take our vacation in the late summer, but
> this year we will take a trip in the fall.

387   Months of the year are capitalized, as are the days of the week.

> Marilee had lunch with Pietro every Thursday for five
> years until this January, when he moved away.
> The trial had to be held on an emergency basis, Monday
> through Sunday, and it did not end until April.

388   Holidays are capitalized.

> The judge's ruling will take effect the day after Thanks-
> giving.
> The Fourth of July picnic will be for staff members and
> their families, but the Christmas party is for staff
> members only.

389 When an organization is named in full in a sentence and subsequently referred to in shortened form either in the same sentence or another, the reference should not be capitalized. Capitalizing the subsequent reference(s) is the practice in some disciplines, but the CR should, for the sake of both simplicity and speed, not make this effort.

> The Sharkey Fishery Company closed its doors two years ago, but the company is reorganizing to reopen this year.

> *Note:* The word *company* in its second occurrence does not need to be capitalized.

> The Department of Health and Human Resources has a huge staff, but the department is generally known as a cordial place to work.
> The University of Vermont has its campus in Burlington, but the university is not the only college in the area.

390 ### References to the U.S. Government

Words that refer to the U.S. government are sometimes capitalized, depending on the preference of the CR's employer or the CR's own preference. The most important consideration is consistency in the use of one or the other style.

> The Federal judgeship was a position he had coveted for years.
> This Republic will not long survive the onslaught of uncontrolled immigration.
> Will our Nation survive another century?

391 ### Personifications

There will be probably few occasions for the CR to deal with personifications, but if such instances do occur, the personification should be capitalized. Personifications occur when human characteristics are given to abstract nouns.

> When Autumn visited our town, she took out her most dazzling hues of red and gold to stun our eyes.
> My favorite season is autumn, but I enjoy spring almost as much.
> I was seized by that villainess Jealousy, who persuaded me to do and say things contrary to my nature.
> His jealousy was becoming a problem to Clarissa.

392   Bills to be considered by the legislature are lowercased.

> The anti-billboard bill is a popular one and will probably become law.
> Senator Judd intends to introduce her education bill this week.

393   Laws, treaties, acts, resolutions, amendments, and formal agreements are capitalized.

> When was the Marshall Plan adopted?
> The Treaty of Versailles ended what war?
> The Civil Rights Act of 1964 was an overdue triumph.

394   Time zones are lowercased except when abbreviated.

> I was happy when daylight savings time was established.
> The launch was scheduled for 9:00 a.m. EST.

395   Names of ships, boats, aircraft, and automobiles are capitalized.

> We like to take the "Miss Suzy Q" out in the lake any chance we have, as sailing is our favorite pastime.
> The "Spirit of St. Louis" can be viewed at the Smithsonian.

396   **Scientific Names**

Capitalize phylum, class, order, family, and genus. Species and subspecies are lowercased.

> The scientific name for the rhesus monkey is *Macaca mulatta*.
> The subclass Rhizopoda consists of creeping protozoans.

Note: Larger divisions (phylum, class, order, family) are not underlined, but genus, species, and subspecies are underlined in CR transcripts.

397   The common, or nonscientific, names of plants and animals are not capitalized unless a proper noun is part of the name.

> The squirrel monkeys are caged in groups of about a dozen.
> His orchids are exquisite.
> I bought my son an Irish setter instead of a poodle.

398 Capitalize names of planets, stars, and constellations except for *sun*, *moon*, and *earth*. When *earth* is used as a planet title, it is capitalized. Do not capitalize generic words.

> The Milky Way galaxy is our own, isn't it?
> We have been watching for Halley's comet every night
> this month.
> Which planet is closer to Earth—Mars or Mercury?

399 Parts of documents are capitalized or lowercased according to their relative size within a document. Major parts (exhibits, volumes, sections, subsections, articles) are capitalized. Minor parts are lowercased (pages, notes, lines, verses). *Paragraph* can be capitalized or lowercased according to the CR's preference (or that of the CR's employer); however, consistency must be maintained throughout the transcript.

  If a particular segment title is written without its number, e.g., chapter, section, paragraph, it is lowercased.

> I do not expect that Article 20 will be approved; it is the
> article sponsored by Davies and Ventura.
> The fourth verse of the poem outlines the author's views
> on war, but verse 11 is explicit also.
> Please refer to page 144 of the monograph.
> Look in Volume 7, Chapter 23, page 477, paragraph 3,
> lines 12-20: There is a glaring error.
> Although the last chapter needs extensive revisions, Chapter 23 is ready.
> There is a clear prohibition of such reimbursements in Section 18, Subsection 43.

400 Capitalize the first word following Q and A in testimony, regardless of whether it is or is not a complete sentence.

> Q. State your name for the record.
> A. My name? Louise.
> Q. Louise what? What is your surname?
> A. Fine. Louise Fine.

401 When referring to the judge, capitalize the word *Court*.

> The Court will now instruct the jury on the law applicable
> to this case.
> If it please the Court, we would like to call a new witness.

402   When referring to a specific court, capitalize; when referring to a type of court, lowercase.

> I am going to take you to court to settle this dispute.
> The U.S. Customs Court will have jurisdiction in this matter.
> He was taken to the Fourth Circuit U.S. Court of Appeals to wait for his father, who was a judge there.
> The court of law in this country is generally respected by the citizens, though not universally.
> The Arkansas Supreme Court will surely rule against him.
> You can pay your ticket at the municipal court.

403   Citations of legal cases are capitalized except for the *v.* or *vs.* (indicating *versus*) and other small words (short prepositions, articles, coordinating conjunctions) that normally would not be capitalized in any title.

> We saw, in *Rich* v. *Underhill Woods & Forests*, a case similar to the one we are hearing today.
> *The State of Michigan* v. *Todd Garilino* will be heard after *Munson* v. *Department of Public Works*.

404   Capitalize names of specific examinations and court documents.

> The jury heard Examination by Attorney Evans on July 18th.
> I refer to Plaintiff's Exhibit No. 2.

> BUT:

> The subpoena was delivered last night.
> We have gathered affidavits from several witnesses and plan to subpoena them, if necessary.

405   Lowercase the word *jury* and the term *members of the jury* or similar terms within the transcript. Capitalize such terms when used as a salutation at the beginning of a jury charge (and set apart from the body of the jury charge).

> Don't you agree, ladies and gentlemen of the jury, that you would have recognized your own brother in such a situation?
> The members of the jury will disregard that last comment.

> BUT: I think, Juror Williams, that you should ask to be relieved of your duties as juror.

406   Capitalize the titles of officers of the court.

> The District Attorney should have made that document available to the Defense.
>
> Please, your Honor, may I make a request?

Note: In the above example, some prefer to capitalize *your* as well as *honor*.

> We will hear the verdict now, Mr. Foreman.

Exercises

A. Capitalize as necessary in the following passage.

Q. When did you last see your brother?

A. Last wednesday night, at peterson's cafe. We were going to go out and buy that boat from Joseph's supervisor.

Q. What boat?

A. A little sailboat called "cat's paw."

Q. Did he say anything to you about mayor smith's daughter?

A. He said that she had flipped out.

Q. Are those his exact words?

A. His exact words? I can give you that. He said, "Ruth Smith has totally and completely flipped out."

Q. Did you know that she suffers from epilepsy?

A. I think I remember father telling him something about that—or was it grandpa? Somebody told him that the mayor's wife had it and so did Ruth.

Q. Was Ruth acquainted with Harley Bloud, jr.?

A. I think Harley worked at telley refinery, inc., while Ruth worked there. Harley was a supervisor there, and Ruth was a chemist. They were both in the greenwich building.

Q. What did you know about Harley?

A. Just that he had a master's in chemistry. I think he got his master of science degree the same year as Ruth did and at the same university.

Q. And what college was that?

A. The university of utah. Harley had a scholarship from the state of utah. Ruth used to work for the city of denver, but she left there to go to the refinery.

B. Correct any capitalization errors.

1. Melvin ("Mr. brain") Ramsey will receive his juris doctorate next month, but he does not want to go into Law. He wants to go into Politics. He is a democrat, and his Father is a big man in that Political Party. He will work as a Professor at the local university for the next couple of years. Although Melvin is White, upper-class, and affluent, he has Liberal ideas and is interested in civil rights.

2. Quincy believed that nature was her counselor, her friend. She refused to take even Aspirin or Tylenol. Her only medicine consisted of herbal remedies and vigorous exercise. She won the Herbert Idelmeyer garden award and was even a rhodes scholar. Quincy placed number 2 in an Orchid-growing contest set up by the New York Botanical Society. The Society presented her with a Certificate. The only other information I have about Quincy is that she is writing a book entitled "Ichabod and Minnie Of the Vale," but I have no idea what this Book discusses. She has written for "The Way Of Nature" as a freelancer and will arrive here in this Courtroom at 8:00 P.M. today. Oh, yes, she is a member of St. Luke's episcopal church located on highway 22.

3. The trial will take place this Autumn. It is based on Marcantel v. Department of Justice. Have you been subpoenaed? Will you tell the court what you know? Has the Government subpoenaed any of your family? It will begin at 9:00 a.m. Eastern Standard Time.

5

Numbers

Language practitioners are sometimes confused when confronted with a choice between using figures or writing out a number. This dilemma is compounded for the CR by the need to record exactly what was spoken without being able to "edit out" awkward arrangements. Rules for number use vary from one profession to the next. The following is a practical guide for determining when a figure should be employed and when the written expression is preferred.

The basic rule is as follows: Write out numbers one through ten; use figures for numbers over ten. There are many exceptions to this rule; however, when the CR can see no other applicable rule or exception, this rule can be relied upon. The CR will be obliged, as always, to follow the preferences of his or her employer and should always strive for consistency within a transcript.

407 Numbers that begin a sentence should be written out unless to do so would be cumbersome, i.e., would require three or more words.

Twenty-three persons were injured in the train derailment.

BUT: There were 23 persons injured in the train derailment.

Q. How much did you earn last year?
A. Thirty thousand.

Q. Do you know the exact number of students enrolled this year?
A. 1,359 is the exact number as of the first day of classes.

408 If an answer in testimony consists of a number alone, the reporter has a choice of words or figures unless, as in the rule above, it would be too long in written-out form.

Q. Can you estimate the number of lost contracts?
A. Twenty. (OPTION: 20.)

Q. What is your area code?
A. 203.

409   Decimals

Use figures for all decimals. For example, if the words actually spoken were "seven point ninety-four," the reporter should write 7.94.

The value of the building was set at $16.9 million.
The animal weighs only 111.34 grams.
The average grade on the exam was 87.6 percent.

Note: If the decimal occurs at the beginning of a sentence, it is still written as a figure. To write it in words interferes with the smooth reading of the transcript.

459.78 persons was the average concert attendance
   last year.
997.40 calories is my average daily intake for this
   month!

410   Use figures to express measurements of length, volume, weight, temperature, etc.

45 miles   10 degrees Fahrenheit
110 volts   4 pounds 9 ounces

Note: It is sometimes acceptable to write out measurements when employing numbers under ten.

Meggan is about five feet tall.
He hopes to grow to be a six-footer.

411   Round numbers can be written in either figures or words, preferably words.

We decided to display two hundred paintings for the show.
A crowd of about two thousand people gathered in the
   streets.
The country's population is about nine million.

412   Write percentages in figures (except at the beginning of a sentence as prescribed by the previous rule).

Ten percent of the nation wanted to avoid an election.
There was 22 percent compliance with the new traffic
   rules.
44.81 percent accuracy is deplorable.

413   Years are never written out, even at the beginning of a sentence. Centuries and decades follow the basic rule.

1978 was a terrible year for me.
The 20th century is now in its last quarter.
The man appeared to be his late 30s. (*thirties* is acceptable)
The fifth century was a time of perpetual warfare.
Music of the '50s and '60s is popular again today.

414 Parts of a document are always identified by figures. This rule applies to pages, sections, chapters, lines, paragraphs, etc.

> The class will cover Chapters 2 through 4 in its next discussion.
> Will the House vote on HR 4522 next month?
> Refer to Section V, page 47, paragraph 2.

415 Numbers in the millions or greater are written as mixed figures and words or, for ten and under, in words only.

Correct

> The population of the area was 22 million.
> He inherited three million dollars from his grandfather.

OPTION: He inherited $3 million from his grandfather.

Wrong

> The population of the area was twenty-two million.
> He inherited $3,000,000 from his grandfather.

416 **Fractions and Mixed Numbers**

Write out fractions; use figures for mixed numbers. This rule is disputed within the industry, as some prefer to write out mixed numbers as they are spoken.

> One fourth of Richard's financial reserves were lost through an IRS ruling.
> He ate $4\frac{1}{2}$ candy bars last night, which accounts for his stomach problems this morning.

Note: The above sentence would be written as follows by those who prefer to write out mixed numbers:

> He ate four and one half candy bars last night, which accounts for his stomach problems this morning.

Note: Some CRs prefer to write fractions exactly as spoken; for example, in the above sentence, if the word *a* were spoken instead of *one*, the fraction would be written as follows: *four and a half candy bars.*

- Amounts less than a dollar are written according to the basic rule with the word *cents*, not with the symbol for cents (¢).

Correct

I found 45 cents on the sidewalk.
The cost of the candy has risen by eight cents.

Wrong

I found 45¢ on the sidewalk.
I found $0.45 on the sidewalk.

- Mixed dollars and cents are written in figures.

I paid $38.42 for my skirt.
Can you lend me the $22.50 I need to pay the bill?

- Dollar amounts that are even are written without decimals.

Correct

My savings account balance at that time was a mere $85, so I could not have paid the $90 to Jeremy by check.
His salary was $1,400 per month.

Wrong

His salary was $1,400.00 per month.

- When several dollar amounts are listed, and at least one requires the use of decimals, the decimal is retained for the sake of consistency.

I have deposited checks in the amounts of $59.10, $74.00, $21.44, $39.71, and $25.00.

- For foreign money, consult the U.S. Government Printing Office Style Manual, foreign money table.

- It is acceptable to use a mixture of words and figures for amounts in the millions and billions.

The shopping center investment is $126 million.
He is worth about $14 million.

- If the word *a* is used with money expressions, it can be employed in the transcript.

I found a hundred dollars in my purse that I didn't know I had!
Can you lend me a 20-dollar bill? (OPTION: $20 bill)

418   Dates are written in accordance with what actually was said. The CR must be exact. If numbers are employed, use the slash to separate the numbers that stand for the month, day, and year.

> We moved into the house on 6/15/79.
> We moved into the house on the 15th of May, 1979.
> We moved into the house on 15 May 1979.
> We moved into the house on May 15, 1979.

419   **Time of Day**

- If *a.m.* or *p.m.* is used with the time, always employ figures.

Correct

We met at the church at 6:35 p.m.

Wrong

We met at the church at six thirty-five p.m.

Also use figures whenever time is mixed hours and minutes, even if *a.m.* or *p.m.* is not used.

> I couldn't believe my eyes when I saw that it was 10:49!

- Military time, or 24-hour time, is written in figures without the use of a colon and is often followed by the word *hours.*

> We were planning to meet at 1800 hours.
> He slept until 1200 hours, unusual for him.

- If the minutes are given before the hour, follow the basic rule.

> The time was precisely 25 till four. (OR: 25 till 4:00)
> He always picked me up at a quarter after seven.
> (OR: quarter after 7:00)

Note: Some prefer the numerical in the above examples, that is, 4:00 and 7:00; if your employer has a preference, follow it. If not, follow your own preference, but be consistent.

- When the word *o'clock* is used, apply the basic rule.

> The accident occurred at six o'clock in the evening.
> I saw him arrive there at 11 o'clock on the dot.

Note: Some prefer to use the numerical here. Others feel that writing "6:00 o'clock" would be like saying "six o'clock o'clock." Thus, there is some disagreement on this matter.

420   **Roman Numerals**

- Because citations often use Roman numerals, the CR should learn to use them with both speed and accuracy.

    This was done in accordance with Title VI regulations.
    Edition VII is the only one that was acceptable.

- Roman numerals with names are not separated from the name they follow by a comma or by any other form of punctuation.

    Napoleon II attempted to invade Mexico; is that correct?
    Richard Alan Ballingham IV will inherit a vast fortune.

421   **Addresses**

- Components of addresses are written in figures. Numbered streets under *11th* may be written out or expressed in figures.

    We drove along Highway 41 for about two hours before getting on Interstate 67.
    She lived at 154-17th Street for five years before moving to Ninth Avenue. (OR: 9th Avenue)

    Note: A hyphen is used in the example above to prevent confusion between the building and street numbers.

    We were supposed to meet in Room 203, but Reva did not show.
    Apartment 3D is now vacant.

    One exception is a street address that begins with the word *one*.

    That sounds like a posh address—One Park Avenue!
    Drive the car around to One Divens Lane.

- Do not use commas in house or building numbers.

Correct

Meet me at 10275 Bluegrass Road.

Wrong

Meet me at 10,275 Bluegrass Road.

422   Always write zip codes, social security numbers, and telephone numbers in figures.

    My name is Willie James, and I live at 34985 Thurmann Street, Chicago, Illinois 60608.
    You can call me during the day at 212/525-8811 or during the evenings at 718/727-4409.

Note: There is no punctuation between the state and the zip code. Note also that the area code is separated from the telephone number by a slash mark.

423   Organization numbers follow the basic rule unless accompanied by *No.* or *Number.*

Q. Were you a member of the Seventh Division in the Pacific?
A. No. I served in the 23rd Artillery.

The First Methodist Church of Denver will be the scene of
the wedding.
Mrs. Simms, did your husband belong to Teamsters No. 6?
Local No. 21 will go on strike at midnight.
Number 5, my son's scout troop, needs a leader.

424   Sessions of Congress also follow the basic rule.

This same issue was debated by the Third Congress.
At the opening of the 97th Congress, we heard from the
distinguished Senator.

425   Successive governments follow the basic rule.

The historian was consumed with interest in the Third
Reich.
The 19th Chang Dynasty was renowned for its promotion
of the arts.

426   **Commas Within Numbers**

The comma should be inserted in figures of a thousand or greater. Some CRs omit the comma in four-figure numbers, but this practice should be confined to numbered documents and addresses.

The House will vote on HR 3411 this afternoon.
They found 1,287 persons in an auditorium that holds
only 950 persons.

Note: Some CRs distinguish between *twelve hundred* and *one thousand two hundred*, which is actually the same number. This distinction would appear to be unnecessary hairsplitting, and to feel obliged to write *12 hundred* rather than *1,200* seems unnecessary; nonetheless, as usual, follow the preference of your firm.

427   When a series of closely related numbers includes some that should be written out and others that should be expressed in figures according to the basic rule, disregard the rule and be consistent.

The children's ages are 4, 9, 12, and 15.
There is a 20-book limit, but I never checked out more
than 5 or 6.

OR: There is a twenty-book limit, but I never checked out
more than five or six.

428   When expressing measured units puts two numbers adjacent to one
another, write out one and use figures for the other. Choose the less
cumbersome arrangement.

We ordered sixteen 24-ounce cans to be delivered Tuesday.

Note: 16 *twenty-four-ounce cans* is more cumbersome and thus not
the version of choice.

James found five 18-pound sacks rather than the standard
order.
We ordered 15 hundred-pound sacks.
We ordered 1500 pound sacks.

Note: The two sentences above mean entirely different things. It is
extremely important for the CR to be accurate in such cases.

429   Exhibits in court are numbered with figures.

Please attach the map as Exhibit 2 to this deposition.
Exhibits 200 through 210 are available for your
examination.

430   Television channel numbers are written as figures.

Channel 2 has the best news, I think.
The broadcast will be carried by Channel 14, WLIC radio.

431   Plurals of figures may be written with or without an apostrophe. The
CR should establish a preference and stick with it.

Your 11's look like 77's.

OPTION: Your 11s look like 77s.

432   Numbers as adjectives should be hyphenated, still adhering to the basic
rule for numbers.

The two-dollar admission price was never a source of
complaint.
The 50-cent piece is rarely used because of its weight.
The 101-year-old woman was spry and vivacious.

Exercise

Correct any errors in the use of numbers in the following:

Q. Where were you going when the accident occurred?

A. I was going to my office. It's Room Five, Twenty-Five Mill Street.

Q. Were you alone?

A. No. My daughters were with me.

Q. What are their ages?

A. Melissa is five, and Alicia is eleven. I also had my neighbor's daughter in the car with me.

Q. How old is she?

A. She is fourteen, I think. She might be fifteen by now.

Q. And were those girls going with you to your office?

A. No. I was dropping them off at a summer camp.

Q. Where was this camp?

A. On Highway Fifty-Five, just off Interstate Ninety-Three.

Q. What is your age, Mrs. Wilke?

A. Thirty-one.

Q. How long have you lived at your present address?

A. I've been there only 4 or 5 months.

Q. Where did you live prior to that?

A. I have a two-year lease on my apartment now.

Q. I asked you where you lived previously.

A. 1011 Timberlane Drive, Memphis Tennessee, 28394.

Q. How long did you live there?

A. 5 years.

Q. What were you carrying in your trunk?

A. I had 10 25-pound sacks of potatoes.

Q. Why were you carrying them?

A. I got them from the farmer who lives out by my parents' house.

Q. Were they all for you?

A. No. I was going to divide them with my 4 sisters and 2 brothers. I got them cheap. The whole bunch only cost me eleven dollars and 50¢.

Q. Were you paying attention to your driving that morning?

A. Sure.

Q. No distractions.

A. Just the radio. I always listen to Channel one twelve on the radio to hear the weather.

Q. Were you carrying a lot of money with you?

A. I had about fifteen hundred dollars with me.

Q. Why were you carrying that kind of cash with you?

A. Two hundred belonged to my office—petty cash. The rest was mine. I planned to deposit 7 hundred and fifty of it in my bank. I had to be at work by eight 30 a.m. I intended to go to my bank on my lunch period.

Q. Where does your husband work?

A. He is deceased.

Q. Where did he work?

A. Construction work out of Local Number twenty-two.

Q. When did he die?

A. April first, 1984.

Q. What is your present annual income?

A. My salary is fifteen thousand five hundred dollars per year at present, but I am due a raise in about 4 months.

Q. Did you receive any insurance benefits as a result of your husband's death?

A. Yes, I did. A hundred thousand dollars.

Q. What bank do you use?

A. The 1st National Bank.

Q. Where is it located?

A. One Grange Street.

6

Abbreviations

As with most punctuation decisions, the CR must rely to a large degree on what is spoken for decisions regarding abbreviations. Actually, abbreviations are used rather infrequently in transcripts with only a few exceptions. When the CR is in doubt, it is generally better not to abbreviate.

433   Write out parts of proper nouns as they are spoken. Do not abbreviate.

Correct

Maple Avenue is five blocks long, but Fir Street is only a single block.

Wrong

Maple Ave. is five blocks long, but Fir St. is only a single block.

Correct

The Chrysler Building is on 42nd Street.

Wrong

The Chrysler Bldg. is on 42nd St.

434   Some titles may be abbreviated if they occur before personal names, including the following:

Singular: Mr., Mrs., Ms., Dr.
Plural: Messrs., Mmes., Mss. (or Mses.), Drs.

Note: *Miss* and its plural, *Misses*, are not abbreviated.

Messrs. Jones and Smith were responsible for the donation of a large amount of money for the hospital fund.
Mmes. Jones and Smith inspired and supported their husbands' interests.
Mss. McNeil and Ryford established new precedents in basketball.
Drs. Crosby and Johnson were held without bond.

Misses O'Flaherty and Niles will be presented at the gala next month.

Mses. O'Riley and Tudor sought an injunction against harassment by that man.

435 Titles that occur in a sentence without a name are written out rather than abbreviated.

I saw my doctor this morning, but he wasn't here for very long.

Tell me, Mister, do you know who I am?

436 Titles other than those listed in Section 434 are not abbreviated.

Captain Tilton will be promoted soon.

I had taken several courses from Professor Chang.

Taylor wrote a letter to the superintendent, but he has received no response other than a call from the office manager.

437 Abbreviations written after names are written with periods.

Martha Cole, D.D.S., is my older sister; didn't you know?

Joseph L. Soames, Ph.D., will conduct the seminar.

438 When part of a name, abbreviate *Jr.*, *Sr.*, and designations such as *III*.

Correct

Mr. Carl J. Davis, Sr., has been appointed to the board.

Bennett Rawlings III has written about a dozen books.

Wrong

Bennett Rawlings the Third has written about a dozen books.

Do not use *Jr.* or *Sr.* in abbreviated form unless the complete name is used.

George Junior does not wish to follow in the footsteps of George Senior by working in the lumber industry.

439 Clipped forms are written without periods.

My math exam was a breeze!

The prep school was exclusive in its reputation only.

My phone was working just fine last night.

Chemistry lab met once a week at 5:00 p.m.

440 Use the ampersand in place of the word *and* only when the company or association employs the ampersand in its official title. If not, write *and* out.

> Johnson & Johnson products are sold in most stores.
> The law firm Lewis, Rawlings & Tiens will represent
>   Mr. Acconia.

Never use the ampersand as an abbreviation for the word *and* within a sentence.

Wrong

The publishers & the printers reached an accord.

441 All-caps abbreviations are written without periods, with few exceptions.

> GMAC (General Motors Acceptance Corporation)
> NEA (National Education Association)
> FBI (Federal Bureau of Investigation)
> CBS (Columbia Broadcasting System)
> WBRZ, WWFL, WXAB, WWL (television and radio
>   stations)

442 The abbreviation for *United States* is written with periods and closed up, that is, with no space between the *U* and the *S*.

> The U.S. delegation will send a representative to the
>   funeral.

443 The abbreviation *D.C.* is written with periods and closed up.

> We had to attend a conference in Washington, D.C.

Note: The U.S. Postal Service specifies a two-letter form without periods (*DC, NY,* etc.) for use with zip-code addresses, but this form should not be used in transcripts.

444 **Time**

A.D. and B.C. are written with caps and periods.
a.m. and p.m. are written with periods and lowercased.

445 Do not abbreviate personal names.

> George (*not* Geo.)
> Benjamin (*not* Benj.—unless, of course, the speaker
>   said *Benj.*)

446 Do not abbreviate parts of geographic names. (Some make an exception of *Saint* and abbreviate it *St.*)

Correct

They lived in Fort Payne, Alabama, for six years.

Wrong

They lived in Ft. Payne, Ala., for six years.

Correct

The papers are filled with news about South Africa.
(NOT S. Africa)
We succeeded in driving up Mount Washington!
(NOT Mt. Washington)
I was planning to drive to Saint Paul. (OR St. Paul)

447   Never abbreviate days of the week or months.

Correct

We met every Tuesday and Thursday in November of
that year.

Wrong

We met every Tues. and Thurs. in Nov. of that year.

448   It is preferred that units of measurement not be abbreviated.

Correct

The room measured 12 feet by 28 feet.

Avoid

The room measured 12 ft. by 28 ft.

Correct

The sample weighed 15 kilos. (OR kilograms, depending on what was spoken)

Avoid

The sample weighed 15 kg.

449   Although it is tempting to abbreviate *Fahrenheit* and *centigrade*, they
should be written out. The word *degrees(s)* should be written out rather
than using the symbol.

Correct

It reached 102 degrees Fahrenheit in Arizona that week.

It reached 102°F in Arizona that week.

Note: *Fahrenheit* is capitalized, but *centigrade* is not.

450   The word *Number* can be abbreviated when used with a numeral.

She lives in Apartment No. 7B.
The winners were Nos. 312 and 411.

Note: If the CR prefers to write out *Number*, this is acceptable, though generally considered less desirable.

451   When used to refer to court cases, *versus* can be abbreviated as *v.* or *vs.*

Do you think this case resembles that of Jones *v.* Battery?

452   **Common Latin Abbreviations**

The abbreviation *e.g.* (meaning "for example"), *i.e.* ("that is"), and *etc.* ("and so forth") are written with periods. The abbreviation *et al.* ("and others") has a period after *al.* but no period after *et*, which is not an abbreviation but the Latin word for *and*. Some CRs prefer not to use *etc.* but to write it out in full: *et cetera*.

The typical New England state, e.g., Massachusetts, is
   steeped in American history.
The informal admonition, i.e., the chancellor's speech, had
   the desired effects on the student body.
The suit was filed by James Reel and the Anderswitt
   Motor Company, et al.

453   Chemical symbols are written without periods. The subscript numbers must be written properly, that is, lower than the letter symbols.

H_2O and CO_2 are the two most prominent products of
   mammalian respiration.

454   *Incorporated* and *Inc.*: Listen to what is said. If *Inc.* ("ink") is what you hear, then write *Inc.*; but if the word is spoken in full, write it out.

455   No period is used when letters are written *as* letters.

Exhibit A was admitted into evidence.
His o's looked like a's.

456   Academic degrees, when abbreviated, are written with periods.

He will have his B.S. by June.
She has given up on her M.A. for now.

Exercise

Correct any errors in abbreviations. If a sentence is correct as is, leave it intact.

1. Samuel Balin, PhD, will address the student body of St. John High School next week.

2. We were in the gym playing basketball, but Paul and Marijo were in the lab working on an assignment.

3. It felt like 100° in the kitchen, but it was only about 85° F.

4. The US flag is flying at half-mast this entire week in recognition of our national tragedy.

5. We lived in Apt. 7, 14 N. Willow St., but our bldg. was sold, so we moved to Giles Boulevard.

6. I met with Msrs. James Jackson and John Rowell on Nov. 9th.

7. The consultation lasted from 10:30 AM until 4:45 PM.

8. I'm being audited by the IRS!

9. We toured the Smithsonian in Washington, DC, but we saw only a small part of the huge place.

10. Do you work for Dr. Morales or for Prof. Hadelmann?

11. Did you report to Lt. Cole, as you were instructed?

12. List your name, address, & telephone number at the top of the page.

13. He is rather tall—about 6 ft. 3 inches, I'd guess.

14. I made an appointment to see my dr. this Fri. afternoon.

15. Hey, Mr., move your car out of my way!

16. Akemi Fujio, MD, was injured this morning in an auto accident out on West Mountain Hwy.

17. He refused to name his son Rutherford J. Adamson, Junior, because he hates the name himself.

18. My favorite radio station is W.U.L.V.

19. He joined the co. in Jan. or Feb. of 1967.

20. Isn't Ft. Walton Beach on Santa Rosa Island?

7
Word Division

The following are a few basic rules about word division. No attempt has been made to present a comprehensive treatment of the subject, as the dictionary is always available. Remember: Word division should be kept to a minimum!

457 Divide a word at the end of a line only when it is absolutely necessary. A page dotted with end-of-the-line hyphens is visually distracting and does nothing to facilitate reading.

458 Never divide words at the ends of more than two consecutive lines.

459 Words are divided according to pronunciation, that is, between syllables. One-syllable words cannot be divided. Watch out for words that appear, at first glance, to have more than one syllable (*jogged, gasped*).

460 Do not divide a word if a one-letter syllable would result (*enough, around, elapse*).

461 A two-letter syllable is acceptable at the end of a line but not at the beginning of the next line. Thus, it would be acceptable to break *en/dure, de/duce,* or *re/view,* but the following breaks are *not* acceptable: *want/ed, church/es, comput/er.*

462 Hyphenated compound words are divided only at the hyphen (*self-/sufficient, cross-/country*).

463 Words containing prefixes or suffixes should be divided between the root word and the prefix or suffix (*joy/fully, un/happy, dis/jointed*).

464 When adding a suffix results in a double consonant, divide the word between those two consonants (*run/ning, occur/ring, beg/ging*).

465 Do not divide words of fewer than six letters (*eject, water, money*).

466   Proper names should not be divided unless there is no way to avoid doing it. In names that use initials, divide after the initials (*W.F.* / *Gillis*, *William F.* / *Gillis*). Divide other names between the given name and the surname (*William* / *Gillis*).

467   Never divide contractions, abbreviations, figures, or abbreviations used with figures (*23 B.C.*).

468   Avoid dividing dates and street addresses.

469   Divide place names between the city and the state (New Orleans, / Louisiana).

470   Never divide the last word of a paragraph or the last word on a page.

Exercise

Assume that the following words occur at the end of a line of type. Decide in what way(s) each should be divided or if it cannot be divided at all. Use slashes to indicate permissible breaks.

alas	touchy	department	reenactment
self-induced	flanked	clothing	announce
enjoyment	elect	saltwater	hazard
emission	can't	breakfast	slammed
should	misused	potential	shouldn't
firsthand	clapping	elusive	assistance

8

Compounds

What would seem to be a fairly simple issue is one that causes many CRs to spend an inordinate amount of time in debate. Should a compound word be written open (as two words), hyphenated, or solid (one word)? In recent years there has been a tendency away from hyphenation, but there are many situations in which the hyphen is still correct. The dictionary can be useful in many cases, but certainly not in all. For one thing, dictionaries sometimes disagree among themselves; for another, many terms are not listed because they are "temporary" compounds created for the specific occasion, e.g., *Maria-like gestures*; and, finally, many terms are sometimes hyphenated and sometimes not, depending on how the compound functions within a given sentence.

The following are some basic rules about compound words:

471 Hyphenate compound adjectives, including those that are "created for the occasion."

> Theirs has been a **long-standing** association.
> Their friendship has been a **here-today-gone-tomorrow** affair.
> Mitchell is a **first-time** offender.
> My **five-year-old son** was terrified of Mason Brown.
> She had that **I-know-something-you-don't-know** look on her face.

472 Use a "suspension" hyphen for two or more adjectives that have the same base and that base is used only once.

> We set both **long-** and **short-term** goals for the committee.
> I applied for either **part-** or **full-time** work at the hospital.

473 Hyphenate written-out numbers from 21 through 99. Do not hyphenate larger numbers.

> **Twenty-seven** is my lucky number.
> **One hundred ten** dollars is a good price for that jacket.
> **Forty-five** people are coming to dinner!

474   Hyphenate fractions in their written-out form when they are used as adjectives. If a fraction functions as a noun, hyphenation is optional.

> A **two-thirds** majority is required for passage of the law.
> She was entitled to **one half** of the property. (OR one-half)

475   Do not hyphenate an adverb that ends with *ly* and the adjective or participle it modifies.

> She seemed to be a **highly motivated** worker.
> Marcus is a **totally devoted** husband to Claire.

476   Do not hyphenate a compound adjective whose first element is the comparative (with *er*) or superlative (with *est*) form of an adjective.

> He was a **clean-shaven**, courteous young man.
> I cannot imagine a **cleaner shaven** young man than
>   Bradley. (comparative)
> Bradley is the **cleanest shaven** young man I have ever
>   met. (superlative)

477   A compound adjective that is hyphenated when it precedes the noun it modifies often is not hyphenated when it functions as a predicate adjective.

> Mr. Dawes is a **well-known** author of regional history
>   books.
> Mr. Dawes, an author of regional history books, is **well
>   known**.
> We need an **up-to-date** report.
> This report is not **up to date**.

478   Sometimes a word is hyphenated to indicate a different meaning from the meaning of the word as written without the hyphen. Such situations involve the prefix *re*.

> We went down to the Caribbean to **recreate** and relax.
> He will have to **re-create** the broken sculpture.
> I could not hear your last **remark**.
> I will **re-mark** the test papers in consideration of the new
>   information.
> Will his **resolve** endure the temptation?
> Your answer is incorrect; you will have to **re-solve** the
>   equation.

479   When a prefix is attached to a proper noun or proper adjective (i.e., one that is capitalized), hyphenate the word.

The **anti-American** sentiment has grown in the past few months.

In your **pre-Timothy** days, you dated a lot of different young men.

480   Do not hyphenate verbs to join them to prepositions, although the same terms, when functioning as nouns or adjectives, are hyphenated.

Can you **follow up** on this report?

BUT: Allen did a **follow-up** report for me.

481   Most prefixed words are written solid, even those that create double vowels.

reenter	coordinate
cooperative	preempt

482   Use a hyphen with the prefix *ex* when it means *former*.

ex-wife

ex-governor

483   Use a hyphen between a prefix and a number.

pre-1960s	post-1975
mid-'80s	

484   Hyphenate terms that are formed by using letters as prefixes.

T-cell	x-ray
S-shape	R-rated movie

485   Exhibit labels employing letters and figures are hyphenated.

Exhibit B-3

Defendant's A-15

486   Hyphens are placed between letters to spell out a word.

Q. How is your surname spelled?
A. Davison. D-A-V-I-S-O-N.

Note: There are no spaces between the letters and hyphens. The letters are caps.

487   A hyphen can sometimes prevent confusion.

He was driving a fast-moving van.

BUT: He was driving a fast moving van.

In her hand she held a strange looking glass.

BUT: In her hand she held a strange-looking glass.

488   Hyphenate to avoid tripling a letter.

Correct

We heard a bell-like sound in the distance.

Wrong

We heard a belllike sound in the distance.

Open, Hyphenated, and Solid Compounds

The following examples show the same terms written differently, depending on the term's function in the sentence. Take careful notice of the differences.

489   **ad-lib • ad lib**

His ad-lib performance was brilliantly entertaining.
I couldn't ad-lib, so I just walked away.
Carlton's speech was done ad lib.

490   **air conditioning • air-condition**

The air conditioning in this building never works.
Papa planned to air-condition our house next summer.

491   **all get out • all get-out**

I wished that they would all get out of my house.
They ran like all get-out when they saw Mickey coming.

492   **all-or-nothing • all or nothing**

His all-or-nothing attitude caused the problems in our friendship.
I didn't care if I received all or nothing for my work; I did it for fun.

493   **all right • alright**

I told him we were doing all right, that he shouldn't worry.

Note: Alright is generally considered incorrect. Use *all right.*

494   **all-time • all time**

   That was his all-time best performance.
   I will remember that day for all time.

495   **all together • altogether**

   The boy stacked the books all together in the corner.
   There were altogether too many people in the room.

496   **already • all ready**

   We have already discussed this issue twice; don't you
   remember?
   The students were all ready for the exam except for
   Patricia.

497   **anyone • any one**

   Mr. Talley would talk to anyone who would listen to him.
   Any one of those books would have been a good choice.

498   **anyplace • any place**

   I don't see your purse anyplace.
   I will meet you at any place or at any time you choose.

499   **anytime • any time**

   "You can do that anytime," he told me.
   I didn't have any time to talk to Miss James.

500   **anyway • any way**

   I didn't want to go anyway.
   I didn't know of any way to get it open.

501   **around-the-clock • around the clock**

   An around-the-clock guard stayed with him even in the
   hospital.
   We studied around the clock for two days.

502   **away • a way**

   I was going away for a week.
   I was hoping to find a way to appease him.

503   **awhile • a while**

Stay awhile with us.
Stay for a while with us.

Note: If the term is preceded by a preposition, use the two-word version.

504   **back out • backout**

I couldn't back out of the garage because of his bicycle.
His backout was a surprise to no one.

505   **back room • backroom**

The back room was sparsely furnished and seldom used.
Backroom activity stopped when Mr. Garcia returned.

506   **backup • back up**

Her backup movements disoriented her assailant.
My backup was Marta, but she was unreliable.
I tried to back up the car.

507   **bailout • bail out**

The fiscal bailout caused jubilation in the company.
His bailout scheme frightened me.
I wanted to bail out my brother, but we had no money.

508   **bareback • bare back**

I rode bareback usually, as I hadn't a good saddle.
He sat out in the sun until his bare back was sunburned.

509   **blackout • black out**

She experienced blackouts now and then.
We would always black out the names on the document.

510   **blastoff • blast off**

The blastoff was scheduled for Tuesday morning, but it
    was cancelled.
I saw Darryl blast off in his new car.

511   **blowup • blow up**

His most recent blowup was his most violent.
I couldn't even blow up a balloon because I was so weak.

512   **breakdown • break down**

His breakdown was shocking to all of us.
I tried to break down the figures into logical categories.

513   **break-in • break in**

The break-in occurred while we were at the theatre.
I lost my key, so I had to break in.

514   **breakout • break out**

The prison breakout sent a wave of fear through the area.
We were just trying to break out of the rut we were in.

515   **breakthrough • break through**

The vaccine was hailed as a medical breakthrough.
I tried to break through his barrier of silence.

516   **breakup • break up**

The breakup of the marriage was hard on Meredith.
She didn't want to break up the meeting, but it was an
emergency.

517   **broken-down • broken down**

His horse was a broken-down nag.
Our furnace had broken down twice that winter.

518   **buildup • build up**

The buildup of arms is of concern to all of us.
He's trying to build up his savings account.

519   **burnout • burn out**

Job burnout is a common problem in our profession.
I thought his enthusiasm would burn out eventually, but I
was mistaken.

520   **buyout • buy out**

The corporate buyout was done secretly and suddenly.
We thought she would try to buy out the boutique.

521   **catch-up • catch up**

Mona's catch-up efforts had her working 18 hours a day.
There was no way I could catch up with Mrs. Pierce.

522   cave-in • cave in

> The cave-in resulted in the loss of 14 lives.
> He would always cave in to his father's wishes.

523   changeover • change over

> The changeover went smoothly, but we disliked
>   Mr. McLaughlin.
> I wanted to change over to the public relations
>   department.

524   checkout • check out

> I just asked her what checkout time was.
> Did he check out before you and Clayton?

525   checkup • check up

> I hadn't had a checkup in three years.
> I didn't appreciate having him check up on me.

526   cleanup • clean up

> The cleanup efforts were halfhearted at best.
> I told Brandon to clean up his room before our guests
>   arrived.

527   comedown • come down

> The job was a big comedown from owning his own
>   business.
> Father shouted at Ben to come down from the roof.

528   coming-out • coming out

> Her coming-out party was a dismal affair.
> We were coming out of the room when he approached us.

529   cover-up • cover up

> The political cover-up was revealed by a fierce journalist.
> He couldn't cover up his lack of skills.

530   crackdown • crack down

> The crackdown had us nervous.
> The new teacher tried to crack down on absenteeism.

531 **crackup • crack up**

The crackup did a great deal of damage to my car.
We told him he would crack up if he didn't slow down.

532 **cutback • cut back**

The cutback on supplies caused hoarding.
I tried to cut back on my expenditures.

533 **downright • down right**

My uncle was downright mean to us!
I studied for six hours, but I just couldn't get my math down right.

534 **drawback • draw back**

The drawback of funds was unethical.
One drawback to his idea was our lack of expertise.
We decided to draw back to our starting point and make new plans.

535 **drive-in • drive in**

I couldn't believe that John had never been to a drive-in theatre.
I couldn't drive in because the snow was too deep.

536 **dropout • drop out**

High school dropouts were uncommon in our community, a fact of which we were all proud.
He told me not to drop out of the program.

537 **dry-rot • dry rot**

If we don't take care, the cloth will dry-rot.
The dry rot caused a loss of several hundreds of dollars.

538 **easygoing • easy going**

I liked his easygoing, friendly manner.
Six years of college were not easy going for me.

539 **ego-trip • ego trip**

It looked as though Helene would ego-trip over the constant compliments from Mr. Hernandez.
The pageant was a much-needed ego trip for Brittany.

540   **everyday • every day**

          In the everyday working world, commuting is common.
          We were in the habit of walking to the park every day at
             sunset.

541   **everyone • every one**

          We invited everyone in the office to the reception.
          Every one of the club members attended.

542   **fallout • fall out**

          The political fallout that followed the investigation had
             profound effects.
          I witnessed the child fall out of the tree.

543   **far-off • far off**

          That far-off look in his eyes warned me of his mood.
          We knew that a layoff was not far off.

544   **first-class • first class**

          First-class accommodations were provided for the
             dignitaries.
          He refused to travel first class because of the cost.

545   **first-degree • first degree**

          She had first-degree burns on her arms and shoulders.
          He was found guilty of murder in the first degree.

546   **flare-up • flare up**

          Barney was told that one more flare-up would cause his
             dismissal.
          I knew that the announcement would flare up discontent.

547   **follow-up • follow up**

          Can you describe the follow-up technique you used?
          If you follow up the lead, you may make a sale.

548   **forasmuch • for as much**

          Forasmuch as most fees are paid, there could be no fiscal
             problems.
          We expected the painting to sell for as much as $2,500.

549 **foul-up • foul up**

> The computer's foul-up caused major problems.
> I was afraid I would foul up the entire operation.

550 **freshwater • fresh water**

> The freshwater harbor is threatened by runoff.
> There was no fresh water for the livestock.

551 **getaway • get away**

> The getaway car was a blue Chevrolet.
> I told him he wouldn't get away with such fraudulent
> practices.

552 **giveaway • give away**

> The grocery giveaway was a huge success and caused a lot
> of excitement.
> I intended to give away all of Matt's clothes.

553 **go-ahead • go ahead**

> He gave me the go-ahead signal.
> I told Walt to go ahead with his retirement plans.

554 **hit-or-miss • hit or miss**

> Arturo's hit-or-miss approach got him fairly good results.
> My plan was at best done hit or miss.

555 **holdup • hold up**

> The holdup frightened everyone in our neighborhood.
> She could not hold up under such pressures.

556 **inside-out • inside out**

> Phil's inside-out clothes didn't bother him.
> Jerry always wore that coat inside out.

557 **knockout • knock out**

> The knockout punch came in the third round.
> Lightning can knock out the entire electrical system.

558 **know-how • know how**

His know-how and my money combined to make us
successful.
I didn't know how to operate the machine.

559 **layoff • lay off**

The layoff wasn't going to affect me or my brother.
The chemical plant had to lay off 55 employees.

560 **layover • lay over**

We had a three-hour layover in Pittsburgh.
We will lay over in London for three days.

561 **long-term • long term**

The long-term effects of the drug are unknown.
Our president was concerned about profits over the long
term.

562 **lookout • look out**

The lookout fell asleep and didn't see anything at all.
I warned Amelia to look out for Craig's tricks.

563 **makeover • make over**

The makeover process required three full hours.
I wanted to make over the filing system.

564 **makeup • make up**

The makeup test was far more difficult.
I couldn't make up all I'd missed.

565 **markup • mark up**

The markup was only 5 percent.
We were planning to mark up the prices after the first of
the year.

566 **middle-class • middle class**

Our middle-class neighborhood was alarmed by their
presence.
We never thought of ourselves as members of the middle
class.

567   **mix-up • mix up**

The mix-up was Mr. Helstrom 's fault.
I made every effort not to mix up the papers.

568   **off-the-record • off the record**

His off-the-record comments were unkind.
I will tell you, but it must be off the record.

569   **payoff • pay off**

The payoff was not the end of the extortion.
I wanted to pay off that debt, but I just couldn't manage it.

570   **pickup • pick up**

The pickup was made on time, but not by me.
No one was willing to pick up the client.

571   **printout • print out**

No printouts may be taken from the office.
We couldn't print out the document because of mechanical failure.

572   **recollect • re-collect**

I cannot recollect when I last saw him.
Because the check was no good, we had to re-collect payment.

573   **recover • re-cover**

We hoped he would recover from his surgery by September.
I wanted to re-cover the sofa in velvet.

574   **release • re-lease**

We refused to release our records to him.
After the tenants moved out, Father decided not to re-lease the carriage house.

575   **roundup • round up**

The roundup was incomplete but was counted a success.
They hoped to round up the kids who were breaking into cars.

576 run-on • run on

She had a habit of writing run-on sentences.
The speech didn't run on as long as we had feared.

577 setup • set up

I realized that the entire situation was a setup to deceive me.
We set up the equipment in Room 26, as instructed.

578 shutdown • shut down

The plant's shutdown caused significant unemployment in the town.
I expected that we would shut down operations for the summer.

579 shut-in • shut in

Old Miss Ames has been a shut-in for 12 years.
We knew it was hopeless to try to shut in every boy who stole hubcaps.

580 sign-off • sign off

Sign-off was at midnight.
We wanted to sign off early that night.

581 snapback • snap back

The snapback came sooner than anticipated.
Jonathan never could snap back after his long illness.

582 sometime • some time • sometimes

Why didn't you call her sometime?
I needed some time to think about the situation.
Sometimes we went to church on Sundays.

583 standoff • stand off

There was a standoff between students and campus police.
I decided to stand off from the group and observe.

584 takeover • take over

The corporate takeover was unexpected.
I had to take over her duties without benefit of training.

585   **turndown • turn down**

> Her turndown altered my plans for the future.
> I couldn't turn down such a lucrative offer.

586   **upper-class • upper class**

> Her upper-class attitude made her unpopular with the staff.
> The upper class seemed to be growing smaller and smaller.

587   **walkout • walk out**

> A general walkout was planned for that Thursday.
> I never dreamed she would walk out on us.

588   **workout • work out**

> We did a 20-minute workout each morning before going to
> the office.
> Lisa didn't believe the plan would work out.

589   **zip-code • zip code**

> Before I took the letters to the post office, I had to zip-code
> them.
> I didn't know what his zip code was, so I asked Dahlia.

Exercises

A. In the sentences below, no hyphens have been used. Insert hyphens where they are needed.

There were two hundred persons present, although we were expecting a much smaller number. Seventy five invitations had been mailed to full time staff members. No family members were supposed to attend the formal attire only dinner, but Mr. Evenna brought along his father in law and his nine year old son. A full figured woman went up to the podium, accompanied by a darkly handsome young man and a strikingly gorgeous, fair haired young woman. The woman was well known to me, but not through my current employment. I knew her through my ex husband. Back in the mid '60s, she used to speak at the university. Her name then was Ora Nielsen. She had a troll like face and a pumpkin shaped body, bright orange colored hair, and lips painted purple. She was an impossible to forget presence wherever she went. Although Ms. Nielsen now had white hair, I was able to recognize her immediately nonetheless.

B. Select and underline the correct version in each sentence: open, hyphenated, or solid.

1. The (breakup, break-up, break up) of the company brought a lot of changes.

2. (Forasmuch, For as much) as he already confessed to the crime, my work is simplified but not finished.

3. I liked to (work out, workout, work-out) at the local gym at least three times a week.

4. Jason was (altogether, all together) baffled by his father's odd behavior.

5. Oscar needed (sometime, some time) to contemplate the proposal before offering his support.

6. We were (already, all ready) to depart when the telephone rang.

7. A few moments passed before Darren was able to (recover, re-cover) from the blow.

8. My criticisms were strictly (off-the-record, off the record).

9. I didn't expect Mr. Arla to (turndown, turn down, turn-down) the proposal, but he did.

10. No (make-up, make up, makeup) exams are given without a valid excuse.

11. His mechanical (knowhow, know-how, know how) made Marco popular around the neighborhood.

12. I told Ivan that there wasn't (anyplace, any place) for him in our organization, not now or ever.

13. An (around the clock, around-the-clock) vigil, though not neces-sary, seemed wise at the time.

14. I couldn't afford to (air condition, air-condition) my car that sum-mer, so I suffered.

15. The (cleanup, clean-up, clean up) was accomplished by a group of students from junior high schools in the area.

16. His (long-term, long term) goals weren't known to me, but my supervisor knew what was going on.

17. We were afraid that Joni would (mix up, mix-up, mixup) the exam scores.

18. The (printout, print-out, print out) didn't supply the information we needed.

19. After Rolph's illness, Gil had to (takeover, take-over, take over) as chairman for the rest of the term.

20. I told Berta that I'd return after (awhile, a while), but she insisted that I remain.

21. Verna thought it would be (alright, all right) if we borrowed the book, but she was mistaken.

22. I didn't expect (anyone, any one) of those gadgets to work properly.

23. Coco and Willis met (everyday, every day) at noon for three years.

24. The plan was never given an official (go-ahead, go ahead).

25. The (walkout, walk-out, walk out) was unsuccessful because so many refused to (cooperate, co-operate).

9

Homonyms and Other Confusions

Naturally, because a CR depends on what he or she hears, homonyms and near-homonyms can be a particularly troublesome area. Many English words that sound exactly alike or somewhat alike have totally different meanings and different spellings as well. It is only through understanding of the possibility of such confusions that the CR can avoid making some embarrassing errors. The following are some word groups that can be troublemakers. This list by no means covers all troublesome word pairs—there are many more. However, the following presents a fairly simplified definition of each that, while not attempting to be comprehensive, gives a basic idea of proper usages.

590   **accede • exceed**

accede (v): to agree, acquiesce, consent

exceed (v): to go beyond a limit or boundary

> The patient will have to accede to his physician's instructions.
> If you exceed the speed limit on Highway 81, you are likely to get caught.

591   **accent • ascent • assent**

accent (n): distinct pronunciation; emphasis; a printing mark to indicate stress of a syllable or pronunciation; (v): to emphasize

ascent (n): advancement; an upward slope

assent (v): to concur or agree; (n): agreement

> His heavy accent made it nearly impossible for the CR to feel confident about the accuracy of his notes.
> Her ascent up the corporate ladder was too rapid for Janet to keep her head about her.
> Did you really expect the judge to assent to your motion?

592   accept • except

accept (*v*): to believe; to take willingly; to receive as one's own

except (*v*): to exclude or exempt; (*prep*): other than

> I will accept the motion and move to table the discussion.
> Except for the final verdict, the jury has completed its work.

593   access • excess

access (*n*): entrance or approachability; (*v*): to gain entrance

excess (*adj*): more than needed or specified; too much; (*n*): superfluity; overindulgence

> How did you gain access to the firm's records?
> The award was in excess of a million dollars.

594   adapt • adept • adopt

adapt (*v*): to adjust to

adept (*adj*): skilled; (*n*): an expert

adopt (*v*): to accept as one's own

> It wasn't easy for Grandfather to adapt to retirement.
> That attorney is adept at getting low bail for his clients.
> The library will adopt a new storage technique next month.

595   adherence • adherents

adherence (*n*): ability or willingness to cling to or support

adherents (*n*): advocates or supporters

> Your adherence to such high standards of behavior is admirable.
> Verna's political adherents number in the thousands.

596   adverse • averse

adverse (*adj*): unfavorable; in opposition (to)

averse (*adj*): reluctant; having a feeling of dislike or dread

> The judgment was adverse to the plaintiff's interests.
> I was averse to having him cross-examined.

597   **affect • effect**

affect (*v*): to influence; (*n*): emotional response (psychology)

effect (*n*): result; (*v*): to cause to happen

> Her wails did not affect me in the least, for I knew they were for show.
> Edward's resignation was the effect of new corporate policies effected by our new chairman.

598   **aid • aide**

aid (*v*): to assist or help; (*n*): assistance

aide (*n*): a person who assists or helps

> Why didn't you aid Miss Detreich when you saw her distress?
> We were planning to hire two new aides for the second floor.

599   **aisle • isle**

aisle (*n*): lane

isle (*n*): small island

> The aisles in the theatre must be at least four feet wide.
> The issue is whether the isle falls within U.S. jurisdiction.

600   **allude • elude**

allude (*v*): to make reference to

elude (*v*): to avoid

> I would prefer it if you wouldn't allude to my former wife.
> He thought he could elude prosecution, and for a long time he did.

601   **allusion • elusion • illusion**

allusion (*n*): reference

elusion (*n*): escape; avoidance

illusion (*n*): an erroneous belief; something unreal

> My lecture was filled with allusions to Greco-Roman mythology.

His elusion of creditors kept him moving from place to place.

I realized that their appearance of affluence was a careful illusion.

602 **altar • alter**

altar (*n*): an elevated structure used in religious ceremonies

alter (*v*): to change or modify

She stood at the altar and announced that the wedding was off.

I knew it was wrong to alter the report, but I felt I had no choice.

603 **aver • avert**

aver (*v*): to affirm

avert (*v*): to turn away from; prevent; turn aside

Can he aver to the truthfulness of his statement?

I averted my eyes so as not to embarrass Peter.

604 **bail • bale**

bail (*n*): security for release of an arrested person; (*v*): to secure a person's release from jail; to extricate; to remove water by scooping or dipping

bale (*n*): a bundle of goods; evil influence; suffering; (*v*): to package in bales

Did you expect the bail to be set so high?

Dad was out there stacking bales of hay in the barn.

605 **bare • bear**

bare (*adj*): uncovered, empty; (*v*): to reveal

bear (*n*): a large mammal; (*v*): to carry; to withstand

I wanted to bare my soul to Laura, but she was pre-occupied.

The scorching sun burned Lisa's bare limbs.

If you can bear to read that long, boring document, let me know what you think of it.

606   bazaar • bizarre

bazaar (*n*): carnival or marketplace

bizarre (*adj*): weird, strange

> The bazaar was a violation of the zoning laws.
> The woman's bizarre behavior alarmed her neighbors.

607   beside • besides

beside (*prep*): near or next to

besides (*adv*): in addition; (*prep*): other than

> Sit down beside me and tell me what happened.
> Besides me and you, who else will work the evening shift?

608   biannual • biennial

biannual (*adj*): occurring twice a year

biennial (*adj*): occurring once every two years

> The board holds biannual planning sessions, one in January and the other in July.
> The association's biennial conventions will be in Denver in 1986; in San Francisco in 1988; in Boston in 1990.

609   bloc • block

bloc (*n*): a group united by some common belief or cause

block (*n*): a city square; a piece of wood; a hindrance; (*v*): to prevent from passing

> The Soviet bloc alleges that a violation of the Geneva Convention has been committed.
> Do you think the board of directors will block the merger?
> He ran 35 city blocks to my house.

610   blond • blonde

blond (*adj*): of a fair or pale color; (*n*): a person with fair hair

blonde (*adj*): of a fair or pale color; (*n*): a girl or woman with fair hair

611   boar • boor • bore

boar (*n*): a wild hog; a male swine

boor (*n*): a crude and distasteful person

bore (*v*): to make a hole or passage; to make weary by being uninteresting; (*n*): a dull or tiresome person or thing

> The curator specified that the European boar would be included in the new display.
> Although handsome, Cal is a boor.
> I can't bore a hole here because the wood is too hard.
> I could never be bored by history; it's my passion.

612 **breach • breech**

breach (*v*): to violate or break; (*n*): a break or interruption; a violation

breech (*n*): the lower or back part of a thing; the part of a gun behind the barrel

> Unauthorized communications are a breach of our contractual arrangement.
> He hit me with the breech of his rifle.

613 **breadth • breath • breathe**

breadth (*n*): width; scope

breath (*n*): air inhaled and exhaled

breathe (*v*): to inhale and exhale; to pause or rest

> The breadth of his interests was impressive.
> She told us she couldn't catch her breath, but we didn't take her seriously.
> We're moving out of the city because we feel we need room to breathe.

614 **brunet • brunette**

brunet (*adj*): of a dark-brown or black color; (*n*): a person with dark hair

brunette (*adj*): of a dark-brown or black color; (*n*): a girl or woman with dark hair

615 **cannon • canon**

cannon (*n*): a big gun; (*v*): to fire a cannon

canon (*n*): a religious regulation

> The child was playing on the old cannon when he began to scream.
> The canon of meatless Fridays was observed by my family.

616   canvas • canvass

canvas (*n*): a rugged cloth

canvass (*v*): to examine or to solicit; (*n*): the act of canvassing

> He always wore an old canvas cloak whenever he took his
> nightly strolls.
> I think it's embarrassing to canvass for votes in one's own
> neighborhood.

617   capital • capitol

capital (*adj*): very serious; excellent; relating to one's assets; (*n*): net
worth; uppercased letter of the alphabet; a city serving as the seat
of government

capitol (*n*): a building in which state or federal legislative bodies meet

> His ideas sound good, but he has no capital to carry out
> his schemes.
> The gunman fired at Senator Garcia from the capitol steps.

618   carat • caret • karat

carat (*n*): a unit of weight for precious stones (variant of *karat*)

caret (*n*): a proofreading symbol used to show where something is to
be added or changed

karat (*n*): a means for measuring the fineness of gold

> The carat weight of the stone was unusually small.
> That omission is too lengthy to be inserted with a caret.
> Until the karat purity of the gold can be measured, I can-
> not offer a price on the jewelry.

619   cellar • seller

cellar (*n*): a basement

seller (*n*): one who sells

> The large cellar could be finished for use as a family room.
> One can never be certain of a seller's honesty.

620   censer • censor • censure

censer (*n*): a container for burning incense, usually in a religious setting

censor (*v*): to examine, looking for something objectionable; (*n*): a person who examines materials for something objectionable

censure (*n*): a reprimand or condemnation; (*v*): to criticize

The censer fell over, but David ran to pick it up.

She worked as a film censor for the government before she came to this country.

Being expelled from her community was an act of censure she found unbearable.

621 **cession • session**

cession (*n*): a concession or yielding

session (*n*): a meeting or meetings

Thanks to her impressive income, we made an unusual cession—unlimited credit.

The legislature will be in session another two weeks.

622 **Chile • chili • chilly**

Chile (*n*): a South American nation

chili (*n*): a sweet or hot pepper; a sauce of chilies and meat (also spelled *chile* or *chilli*)

chilly (*adj*): cool

The president of Chile will be in Washington next week.

Most cooks in the American Southwest know how to make chili.

The weather was too chilly for swimming.

623 **chord • cord**

chord (*n*): several tones sounded together

cord (*n*): several strands of material twisted together; electrical cable; ribbed fabric; an anatomical part resembling a cord; (*v*): to pile up wood in cords; to bind with a cord

She always messed up the G chord in that musical piece.

Our firm is best known for its medical-quality surgical cord.

624 **cite • sight • site**

cite (*v*): to refer to or quote from; to call upon officially to appear

sight (*n*): a spectacle; a panoramic or unusual view; vision; judgment; (*v*): to look at; to take aim

site (*n*): a place or location

He cited examples of several similar cases.

I looked around the street where we were to meet, but I couldn't catch sight of her.

We had selected a site for the shopping center, but the seller backed out of the deal.

625   **coarse • course**

coarse (*adj*): rough, crude, of inferior quality

course (*n*): route; planned program of instruction; (*v*): to traverse; to pursue

The fabric he used was too coarse.

The course of the parade was changed at the last minute.

626   **complement • compliment**

complement (*n*): something that makes whole or satisfies; (*v*): to be complementary to

compliment (*n*): an expression of praise or admiration; (*v*): to offer approval or praise

Vegetable proteins can complement each other to produce nutritious meals.

Because Miss Thierrot seldom complimented anyone, I was thrilled by her words of praise.

627   **conscience • conscious**

conscience (*n*): an awareness of morality

conscious (*adj*): aware

It seemed to me, from our long discussions, that he had never developed a conscience.

She had no conscious memory of what had transpired, although she had witnessed the crime.

628   **consul • council • counsel**

consul (*n*): a government official appointed to live in a foreign country and to represent the appointing country

council (*n*): an assembly; governing body

counsel (*n*): advice; an attorney; deliberation; (*v*): to advise

The State Department will appoint a new consul immediately after his resignation.

The neighborhood's safety council adopted the police chief's recommendations.

After careful consideration and counsel of friends and relatives, I decided to leave.

629   **core • corps • corpse**

core (n): central part of something

corps (n): a group of persons having the same occupation, activity, or direction; military subgroup

corpse (n): a dead body

> The university's core courses include several of the social sciences.
> The U.S. Marine Corps has a recruiting office near that building.
> A corpse was discovered in the woods behind Uncle Jake's farm.

630   **descent • dissent**

descent (n): lineage or ancestry; a downward slope; attack; derivation

dissent (v): to have a different opinion; (n): a difference of opinion; ideological nonconformity

> My descent into depression was a slow but painful one.
> Political dissent forced Ms. Caldra to withdraw from the race.

631   **die • dye**

die (v): to end biologically; to expire; (n): singular of *dice*

dye (v): to color; (n): coloring matter

> He threw the die and got a snake-eye, the winning roll.
> I thought I would die from anxiety.
> I didn't recognize Kristin because she had dyed her hair red and lost more than 25 pounds.

632   **discreet • discrete**

discreet (*adj*): exercising careful judgment

discrete (*adj*): made up of distinct or unconnected elements

Because of her public role, my mother was obliged to be discreet.

The problem will be easier to solve if it is broken into discrete parts.

633   **discus • discuss**

discus (*n*): a heavy disk thrown as a test of strength and skill

discuss (*v*): to explore a topic in conversation or writing

The discus has been used since the time of the Greeks.

They discussed selling the property, but there was no agreement.

634   **elicit • illicit**

elicit (*v*): to bring out; to derive

illicit (*adj*): forbidden or disapproved

She was known for her ability to elicit brilliant performances from her students.

He swore that there was nothing illicit about his behavior with her.

635   **emerge • immerge**

emerge (*v*): to rise; to become clear

immerge (*v*): to plunge into; to become intensely involved

The details of the contract will emerge at the board meeting next week.

Ms. Gorbea immerged herself in the project to the extent that we seldom saw her.

636   **emigrate • immigrate**

emigrate (*v*): to leave one's native country to live elsewhere

immigrate (*v*): to move to a country that is not one's native country

He made the decision to emigrate rather than live under the new government.

His immigration to the United States came five years after his wife's death.

637   **eminent • imminent**

eminent (*adj*): outstanding; famous

imminent (*adj*): about to occur

My sister is an eminent psychologist in Chicago.
His election was considered imminent.

638   **envelop • envelope**

envelop (*v*): to enclose or surround

envelope (*n*): a wrapper or covering

> I watched the clouds envelop the sun and knew a
> storm was coming.
> We always used the padded envelopes to mail the
> film.

639   **exercise • exorcise**

exercise (*v*): to use; to exert; to use regularly to strengthen or develop;
(*n*): the act of bringing into play; carrying out as per an agreement;
bodily exertion for physical fitness

exorcise (*v*): to expel; to free oneself of

> I was surprised when he didn't exercise his right to appeal.
> She began a rigorous program of exercise that she was not
> fit to do.
> He hoped his new life would exorcise his memories of the
> past.

640   **faint • feint**

faint (*v*): to lose consciousness; (*n*): sensation of dizziness and weak-
ness; (*adj*): weak; cowardly; dim

feint (*n*): something feigned; (*v*): to make a pretense of

> Much of the trial's substance hinges on whether she
> fainted or only pretended to do so.
> His feint didn't work on this particular opponent.

641   **farther • further**

farther (*adv*): at a greater distance

further (*adj*): additional; (*v*): to advance or promote

> We had driven along Old Port Road farther than five miles
> when we realized something was wrong with the car.
> I had to have further information before I could make a
> decision.

642   **faze • phase**

faze (*v*): to upset or disturb

phase (*n*): period, stage, or cycle; (*v*): to introduce or carry out in stages

His ranting didn't faze Martha, but it drove Jude mad.
Those procedures would be phased out with the new
administration.

643   **flair • flare**

flair (*n*): an ability or talent; style

flare (*n*): a glaring light or fire; a sudden outburst; (*v*): to shine; to
become angry or excited

Mona just didn't have a flair for fashion.
His temper flared irregularly but violently.

644   **flaunt • flout**

flaunt (*v*): to display

flout (*v*): to scorn; to treat contemptuously; (*n*): an insult

She flaunted her success before her sister.
Edward flouted the association's rules and principles with
an embarrassing regularity.

645   **foreword • forward**

foreword (*n*): a preface or introduction

forward (*adj*): bold; advanced; in front; (*v*): to send; to promote; (*adv*):
in the direction of the front; (*n*): in sports, a player who is at the
front of the formation

The foreword of Hogan's book was to be written by his
associate, Warren Bourgeois.
It was hard to tell whether he was being forward or merely
friendly.

646   **formally • formerly**

formally (*adv*): done in traditional style

formerly (*adv*): previously

He formally withdrew from the campaign after the
diagnosis.
Lydia Ramos was formerly associated with an electronics
company in California.

647   foul • fowl

foul (n): a breaking of a rule; (adj): distasteful, offensive; obscene; dirty;
(v): to rot; to obstruct; to make dirty

fowl (n): any variety of bird

Rita felt that her home was fouled by his very presence.
Oscar hunted fowl, but he refused to hunt deer or moose.

648   gilt • guilt

gilt (adj): covered with gold; (n): gold or something that seems to be
gold

guilt (n): a consciousness of having done wrong; culpability

The only items in the estate that interested me were the
gilt-edged picture frames.
Her guilt seemed obvious from the onset of the trial.

649   gorge • gouge

gorge (v): to fill to capacity; (n): a narrow canyon

gouge (v): to shamefully overcharge; to poke; to scoop out a groove
or channel; (n): a groove; a chisel

Werner gorged himself on pastry and ice cream until he
was sick.
I told her she had gouged my eye, but she turned away.

650   grate • great

grate (n): a framework of parallel or crisscrossed bars used for various
purposes; (v): to annoy; to rub noisily; to rub into small pieces

great (adj): something significant or large; distinguished; grand

When Horace dropped his silver dollar down into the
grate, he screeched.
The infant's crying clearly grated on Aunt Patrice's nerves.
His great love of the White Mountains induced him to
build a cabin up there.

651   grisly • grizzly

grisly (adj): causing horror or distaste

grizzly (n): species of bear; (adj): somewhat gray

The grisly scene caused Jenny to run out of the theatre.
A grizzly-haired old man was mumbling something and
pulling on her sleeve.

652 **hangar • hanger**

hangar (*n*): a structure designed for storage, usually of aircraft

hanger (*n*): a device from which something is suspended

> The mayor announced that the municipal airport would
> have additional hangar space.
> I never put my clothes on hangers but folded them instead.

653 **heal • heel**

heal (*v*): to mend; to bring back to health

heel (*n*): the back of the foot; the bottom part of something; a contemptible person

> The cut on Linda's arm just wouldn't heal.
> Although I liked Ned at first, I learned soon enough that
> he was really a heel.

654 **hew • hue**

hew (*v*): to shape or cut with blows

hue (*n*): color; aspect

> He used a small hatchet to hew the wood.
> Those subtle hues were quite pleasant.

655 **hoard • horde**

hoard (*v*): to store up; to keep to oneself; (*n*): that which is hoarded

horde (*n*): a large crowd; a swarm

> Our hoard of dehydrated food was to feed us while we
> were camping.
> A horde of angry people stood outside our building, but
> there was no violence.

656 **incite • insight**

incite (*v*): to move to action; to stir up

insight (*n*): discernment; ability to see clearly

> Mr. Torres' speech was intended to incite the workers to
> strike.
> Tien's grandmother often offered insight and advice to us
> when we had problems.

657   **ingenious • ingenuous**

ingenious (*adj*): unusually clever

ingenuous (*adj*): natural; without guile

> His ingenious scheme made us a small fortune in a short time.
>
> Although Edith seemed ingenuous, she could be manipulative and deceitful.

658   **lead • led**

lead (*v*): to guide or direct; to be first; to open or begin; (*n*): the one in front position; a clue; a metal

led (*v*): past tense and past participle of the verb *lead*

> He was the lead singer for the group for two years.
>
> I can lead you through those difficult passages.
>
> I needed a No. 2 lead pencil to take the examination, but all I had was a pen.
>
> She led us to the place where she found the stolen goods.

659   **lesser • lessor**

lesser (*adj*): smaller, less, or less important

lessor (*n*): someone from whom one leases something

> I believed that lying to Ivan was the lesser of two evils.
>
> The lessor of our apartment lived out of state.

660   **liable • libel**

liable (*adj*): responsible

libel (*n*): unflattering, malicious, or damaging portrayal (written or printed)

> Zed knew he was liable for the damages inflicted by his son.
>
> I didn't think the comments in my letter could be considered libel!

661   **lightening • lightning**

lightening (*n*): relieving; lessening

lightning (*n*): atmospheric electricity

> My responsibilities were to undergo a lightening within the year.
>
> The lightning must have hit our barn to start the fire.

662 loath • loathe

loath (*adj*): reluctant

loathe (*v*): to detest

> I knew he would be loath to fire her, but it seemed
> inevitable.
> Mr. Wollin loathed his brother, and we were all aware of
> that animosity.

663 loose • lose

loose (*adj*): not firmly attached

lose (*v*): to suffer the loss of; to fail to win; to get rid of

> The screw was loose, but I had no tools with me.
> He knew he would lose his role if he missed rehearsal.

664 medal • meddle • metal

medal (*n*): a piece of metal given for commemorative or religious purposes or as an award

meddle (*v*): to interfere in matters not one's concern

metal (*n*): any of various opaque, durable, ductile substances that are
good conductors of heat and electricity

> He treasured his athletic medals and would never have
> thrown them out.
> Melanie disliked her mother's meddling in Jason's financial
> affairs.
> The name of one of the metals was misspelled throughout
> the document.

665 monetary • monitory

monetary (*adj*): having to do with money

monitory (*adj*): serving to warn

> The committee had no influence in the shaping of
> monetary policies.
> The monitory tone of his letters concerned me.

666 naval • navel

naval (*adj*): pertaining to a navy or ships

navel (*n*): a depression in the middle of the abdomen; a central point

A nation's strength is often measured by the size of its
naval force.

My aunt told us to use mineral oil to clean the baby's
navel.

667   **palate • palette • pallet**

palate (*n*): the roof of the mouth; sense of taste

palette (*n*): a board on which an artist mixes colors

pallet (*n*): a mattress or temporary bed; a portable platform; a wooden
instrument with a flat blade

> His palate became more sophisticated after he had lived
> in New York City and experienced its wealth of
> restaurants.
> The artist's palette held only various shades of the same
> color.
> While they were staying with us, Betty and Emma slept
> on pallets in my room.

668   **passed • past**

passed (*v*): past tense of *pass*

past (*adj*): bygone; (*n*): a time that has gone by; (*prep*): beyond; (*adv*):
at an end

> Only 15 percent of the students passed the examination!
> I passed the drugstore on my way home each evening.
> His past affiliations were unknown to me at that time.
> We drove past Eleanor's house, but there were no lights
> on inside.

669   **peak • peek • pique**

peak (*n*): the high point or top; (*v*): to bring to a conclusion or reach
the maximum; (*adj*): at or near the maximum

peek (*v*): to glance; to look furtively; (*n*): a brief look

pique (*v*): to cause resentment or anger; to arouse; (*n*): resentment;
wounded pride

> The mountain's peak was rocky and strewn with debris.
> The feud peaked with Nell's decision to leave.
> I peeked through the curtains to see if he had left.
> Millie was piqued by my failure to telephone her.

670   **peal • peel**

peal (n): a loud sound; (v): to give out peals; to resound or ring

peel (n): the rind or skin of a fruit; (v): to remove the outer layer

> The peal of the church bells occurred only at noon on
> Sundays.
> The orange peel lying on the floor caused Gretchen to slip.
> She peeled 300 labels from cans.

671   **pedal • peddle • petal**

pedal (n): a foot lever; (v): to use pedals; (adj): pertaining to the foot

peddle (v): to offer for sale

petal (n): the part of a flower that is usually the colorful part

> The bicycle pedal fell off, causing Addie to stop riding.
> The steep grade of the hill caused us to pedal harder than
> we had ever had to before.
> Greg was anxious to peddle his goods, and his enthusiasm
> was catching.
> I nearly cried when the petals fell from the roses.

672   **peer • pier**

peer (v): to look closely and searchingly; (n): someone of equal status

pier (n): a supporting structure; a structure on or in the water

> I peered at the address on the envelope but couldn't make
> it out.
> Matt felt he couldn't communicate with his peers.
> For three hours we sat on the pier without speaking.

673   **personal • personnel**

personal (adj): having to do with a person; private

personnel (n): employees, staff

> I told him I wouldn't discuss my personal life at work.
> Our personnel problems climaxed with the strike.

674   **plaintiff • plaintive**

plaintiff (n): the complaining party or parties in a litigation

plaintive (adj): expressive of sadness or suffering

> The plaintiff wasn't prepared to prove his accusations.
> The plaintive wails seemed to come from the wooded area.

675   precedence • precedents

precedence (n): something given higher importance; preference

precedents (n): actions of the past that may serve as an example or rule to justify similar actions in the future

> Precedence will be given to educational needs.
> Precedents do not suggest a large settlement in this case.

676   principal • principle

principal (adj): most important; (n): a person of leading authority; a capital sum; the person primarily responsible

principle (n): a law; a doctrine; a code of conduct

> The principal concern was Mother's health.
> Ms. Ingra was appointed principal of the junior high school.
> She was considered a woman of high principles.

677   rational • rationale

rational (adj): able to think logically

rationale (n): an explanation or reason

> Our decision to move seemed like a rational one at the time.
> His rationale for buying that kind of house had to do with tax benefits.

678   reign • rein

reign (n): the time during which one has power; sovereignty; (v): to rule

rein (n): a strip of leather used to guide a horse; something that controls or guides; (v): to stop or slow down

> Father reigned over the entire family like an emperor.
> I pulled at the reins, but the horse continued to gallop wildly through the field.
> He kept a tight rein on our finances.

679   respectfully • respectively

respectfully (adv): in a manner showing respect or deference

respectively (adv): in the order named

> Rolinda spoke to Aunt Vera respectfully, but John was shouting.

The cost of the trips to Paris and Rome was $950 and
$875, respectively.

680   **right • rite • wright • write**

right (*adj*): correct; (*n*): privilege; (*v*): to make amends for; to restore;
(*adv*): correctly; immediately

rite (*n*): a ceremony

wright (*n*): a suffix meaning *worker*

write (*v*): to compose

> We were just trying to right all the wrongs we'd done.
> Marriage rites differ from culture to culture.
> The playwright filed suit alleging copyright violations.
> He couldn't write, but he wanted to be a novelist.

681   **role • roll**

role (*n*): capacity; function

roll (*n*): a rotating movement; a list of names; (*v*): to rotate on an axis;
to turn over and over

> The role of executive assistant is unclear to me.
> The roll was called during the first five minutes of class.

682   **rote • wrote**

rote (*n*): a routine, mechanical way of doing something; (*adj*):
mechanical

wrote (*v*): past tense of *write*

> His rote recitation held no emotion or understanding and
> moved no one.
> Kane wrote to the admissions board three weeks before he
> contacted you.

683   **shear • sheer**

shear (*n*): one blade of a pair of shears; (*v*): to cut or trim

sheer (*adj*): thin or transparent; steep; pure; (*v*): to deviate or turn aside

> Dr. Marlowe dropped the shears to the floor when she saw
> Beryl's condition.
> I had to shear off about a quarter of the excess.
> She was wearing a long, sheer robe.

684   sleight • slight

sleight (*n*): skill; deceitful craftiness; trick or strategem

slight (*adj*): slim; frail; insignificant; (*n*): an act of discourtesy; (*v*): to neglect

> She interpreted his early departure as a sleight to avoid further questioning.
> He was a man of slight build and dark complexion, perhaps 30 years old.

685   stationary • stationery

stationary (*adj*): unmoving or unchanging

stationery (*n*): writing paper and envelopes

> The automobile remained stationary in front of my house for several days.
> I recognized her stationery if not her handwriting.

686   taught • taut

taught (*v*): past tense of *teach*

taut (*adj*): tight

> She taught me to speak French, and I taught her to play the piano.
> My nerves were taut as I waited for his arrival.

687   throe • throw

throe (*n*): violent spasm

throw (*v*): to toss; (*n*): the act of tossing

> The child appeared to be in the throes of agony.
> His throw was too high for anyone to catch.

688   timber • timbre

timber (*n*): lumber

timbre (*n*): a distinctive quality of sound

> Timber prices were soaring, and we were concerned for our business.
> Her timbre in the Schubert songs was rich and lovely.

689   **treaties • treatise**

treaties (*n*): formal agreements

treatise (*n*): a written discussion

> It is expected that the treaties will be signed within the
> week.
> Professor Sanda's treatise on the ethics of capitalism will be
> published.

690   **troop • troupe**

troop (*n*): a group of soldiers; a collection of people or things; (*v*): to
walk, especially in a group

troupe (*n*): a company, especially theatrical; (*v*): to travel in a troupe

> The scout troop planned a camping trip near Lake Carrill.
> He was working on a history of the German theatre
> troupe.

691   **trustee • trusty**

trustee (*n*): someone to whom something is entrusted; one who legally
administers on behalf of another person

trusty (*adj*): dependable; (*n*): a trusted person who is granted special
privileges, especially a convict

> Miss MacManus was shocked to learn that she had been
> appointed trustee.
> Ben always called Peter his trusty sidekick.

692   **waive • wave**

waive (*v*): to surrender voluntarily

wave (*n*): a swell of water; a curve; a surge of emotion; a hand gesture; (*v*): to flutter; to gesture in greeting or farewell

> He waived his right to an attorney.
> He waved farewell to us as he drove away.
> The wave dumped a huge quantity of water into our small
> boat.

Exercise

Select and underline the correct word or words in each of the following sentences.

1. Hayley, an (ingenious, ingenuous) young woman, trusted Lenny and told him her personal business, which he later used against her.

2. The proposed (cite, sight, site) for the municipal auditorium has stirred up a controversy.

3. Try as I might, I could find no (insight, incite) into the problem, not even from talking with my best friend, C.J.

4. This arsonist has (alluded, eluded) the law until now.

5. My (conscience, conscious) demanded that I come forward with everything I knew about the crime.

6. He (cited, sighted) numerous (precedence, precedents) for the action.

7. What a (capital, capitol) idea!

8. Thomas made no secret of the fact that he was (adverse, averse) to your plan.

9. Morris has had (monetary, monitory) problems ever since he lost his job last year.

10. The (ascent, assent) to the waterfalls is steep and rocky.

11. We tried to (boar, boor, bore) holes in the brick wall to mount the painting.

12. (Censer, Censor, Censure) meant the end of the Senator's career.

13. This applicant's salary demands (accede, exceed) the company's financial ability.

14. Was such disclosure considered a (breach, breech) of confidence?

15. Manfred's (boarish, boorish, borish) manners caused his wife great embarrassment.

16. The patient's (breath, breathe) was irregular and faint.

17. We walked over to the (capital, capitol) building together at 3:15 p.m.

18. Did Mr. Gray give his (ascent, assent) to these changes?

19. I just couldn't (bare, bear) to see his humiliation; I left the room.

20. Jamie offered to (canvas, canvass) the eastern part of town so that the quota might be met.

21. The attorney frequently (alluded, eluded) to Jim Mason's past record.

22. The (cannons, canons) of the church have been challenged before.

23. Jacob's idea, hailed as an (ingenious, ingenuous) achievement, saved the company a bundle of money.

24. The orchestra was (lead, led) by a last-minute substitute that evening, causing an uneven performance.

25. My in-laws never tried to (meddle, medal, metal) in our marital problems.

26. Lee's cousin was (loath, loathe) to testify against a member of his family.

27. Willie and I (pealed, peeled) potatoes until our hands were sore.

28. The (plaintiff, plaintive) sounds may have been from someone who was injured or sick.

29. My grandmother (hoarded, horded) family photographs and memorabilia, allowing no one to see her treasures.

30. The kids slept on (palates, palettes, pallets) in the basement.

31. I couldn't resist taking a (peak, peek) into the newly decorated room.

32. Betsy's constant complaining (incited, insighted) discontent in the entire office staff.

33. Harold's interest in astronomy (peaked, peeked, piqued) and then declined.

34. Calling Ned all those awful names could be considered (liable, libel).

35. The interest payable on the loan was twice the amount of the (principal, principle).

36. The sun shone on the (medal, meddle, metal), blinding me for a moment.

37. Barlow couldn't (pedal, peddle, petal) up the hill to our house.

38. The room was done in various (hews, hues) of pink and green.

39. A (hoard, horde) of people gathered at the hall of justice to see the infamous criminal.

40. Kane (flaunted, flouted) his wealth rarely, but he was outrageous when he did.

41. My problems seemed to (envelop, envelope) me in a cloud of gloom and depression.

42. Although I knew of his resignation weeks before it occurred, Franklin's announcement was not made (formally, formerly) until June.

43. I (gorged, gouged) myself on pizza until I felt sick.

44. Maria's (flair, flare) for floral design was useful to us.

45. I had intended to (cite, sight, site) several authorities in my argument.

46. We were never (conscience, conscious) of any subversive activities.

47. Jeanne (fainted, feinted) an attack on her brother and then slugged Carmine.

48. I had to get permission from Jane Dunham to give Mr. Clary (access, excess) to the files in my office.

49. Although he is a popular young man, Mack's suspension is considered to be (eminent, imminent).

50. We watched a (grisly, grizzly) horror movie on cable television.

51. The headmaster demanded strict (adherence, adherents) to the established code of conduct.

52. The student (council, counsel, consul) will meet every Tuesday afternoon; class representatives were elected last month.

53. Maynard (gorged, gouged) a hole into the wood with a screwdriver.

54. Ben felt like a (heal, heel) when he told Jennifer the bad news.

55. Cory was finally (emerging, immerging) from his depression, but then a disaster occurred that put him back down again.

56. The chairman certainly pulled the (reigns, reins) on his ambitions.

57. The (shear, sheer) fabric of the curtains enabled us to see what was going on in the dining room.

58. Charita's personal (stationary, stationery) was an elegant ivory parchment trimmed with gold.

59. Professor Behrmann seldom called (role, roll) in his morning classes.

60. Tony never (flaunted, flouted) his bankroll at work, but it was a different story when he went out in the evening.

61. The (elicit, illicit) photographs were published years after they were taken.

62. Because there was an (access, excess) of office supplies, no orders were made for a couple of months.

63. Although no insult was intended, Miss Emmanuel felt we had (sleighted, slighted) her and her family.

64. We tried to secure the trunk with a piece of (chord, cord), but it was hopeless.

65. His (eminence, imminence) in his field is evidenced by the number of awards he has won.

66. All of my (allusions, elusions, illusions) about Josh's character were shattered abruptly that night.

67. When my brother was tense or angry, he'd go out to the field and (bail, bale) hay or do something else physically rigorous.

68. Green (die, dye) dripped all over the carpet and left ugly stains.

69. No one expected Robert to (accede, exceed) to his former wife's enormous financial demands.

70. (Adverse, Averse) publicity disturbed the candidate for mayor.

71. Lunch consisted of (chili, chilly), crackers, and soda.

72. Hal had (emerged, immerged) himself in his work.

73. Jena felt that her intellectual development had been (stationary, stationery).

74. The film was rated as obscene by the (censers, censors, censures).

75. Dr. Mim's (consul, council, counsel) to Jan was that she should go ahead.

76. The book's (foreword, forward) helped me understand what the author was attempting to say.

10

The Final Product

693   **Paragraphing**

The purpose of paragraphing is basically the same as that of punctuation: to make reading easier, clearer, and smoother. A new paragraph signals a shift or change of some kind. Often a speaker will go on at considerable length—in jury charges, opening and closing remarks of the attorneys, etc. The CR should break up such long passages into smaller units, or paragraphs, for the reader's sake. A page of unbroken lines appears forbidding.

Although there is no ironclad number of lines or sentences that comprise the ideal paragraph, some general guidelines can be set forth. A single paragraph should run no longer than eight to ten lines and no shorter than four to five lines. One-sentence paragraphs are considered undesirable. There are, of course, situations in which they cannot be avoided.

Often a speaker seems to ramble on and on about a single subject. Even in long recitations of this kind, there are natural breaks—shifts in topic, tone, and approach. The CR should be alert to these logical points for paragraphing.

Some situations demand paragraphing regardless of the length of the resulting paragraphs. For example, during Q and A, it is common for another speaker to enter: the Court may ask a question or make a comment, or another attorney may raise an objection. This is called *colloquy*. The CR should start a new paragraph for each new speaker and for each new person addressed.

694   **Enumerations**

Enumerations can be handled in one of two ways. A short enumeration is incorporated into the body of the sentence that introduces it; a lengthy enumeration is set off from straight text, with each item in a separate paragraph.

The second format is commonly used for courtroom material like the following:

1. Components of the jury's decision
2. Terms of a stipulation
3. Grounds for making a motion
4. The judge's opinion
5. The judge's charge

Note that the items in a lengthy enumeration are not followed by periods unless they are complete sentences.

Enumerations may occur numbered or unnumbered. For those that are numbered, if the speaker used ordinals (*first, second, third,* etc.), write out the words rather than using numerals. If the speaker used *one, two, three,* etc., use figures.

> First, you do not have your facts straight; second, you are misinterpreting the applicable law; third, you are jeopardizing your own reputation and career.

> BUT: I have to say to you that (1) you do not have your facts straight; (2) you are misinterpreting the applicable law; and (3) you are jeopardizing your own reputation and career.

Remember to use semicolons to separate items in an enumeration when the enumeration is incorporated within the sentence.

695   **Spacing**

The following are a few rules for spacing correctly within your document:

1. Space twice after each sentence, whether the sentence ends with a period, a question mark, an exclamation point, or a quotation mark.
2. Space twice after a colon, except in expressions of time (e.g., *4:35 p.m.*) and in citations (e.g., *Genesis 5:12*).
3. A dash is written by typing two unspaced hyphens. There is no space before the hyphens and none after—unless the dash occurs at the end of a sentence.
4. Do not space before or after a virgule, except when it is used to separate lines of poetry.
5. Space once after a semicolon and once after a comma.
6. Do not space before a comma, semicolon, colon, closing quotation mark, closing parenthesis, or period.
7. Do not space after an opening quotation mark or after an opening parenthesis.
8. For long quotations, indent an additional five to ten spaces from the left margin. Some use an indention of five to ten spaces on

the right side as well. Use an opening quotation mark at the beginning of each new paragraph, but use a closing quotation mark only at the end of the final paragraph of the quotation, not at the end of each paragraph.

696   **Proofreading**

Proofreading your work is one of the most important steps in producing a first-class document. Although it is sometimes difficult to put forth the effort, this step deserves full attention and extreme care.

There are basically two types of errors: content errors and mechanical errors. Content errors are problems with logic—when the words are technically correct but do not make sense. Lack of consistency is another kind of content error. Mechanical errors include typos, punctuation problems, capitalization errors, and mistakes in formatting.

Because the two types of errors are so fundamentally different, it is highly advisable that the work be read at least twice—once for content and once for mechanical errors. Reading for content means making sure the words make sense. This process is completely different from searching for mechanical errors. The following are a few suggestions for effective proofreading:

1. Proofreading demands concentration and thus should be done at a slower speed than one's normal reading speed.
2. Some CRs find it helpful to use a ruler under the line being proofread to increase concentration.
3. When pondering over punctuation, remember that less is usually, though certainly not always, preferable to more.
4. Do not hesitate to use reference materials to the degree necessary (see Unit 12). A good dictionary is an indispensable tool for the CR.
5. Use the American rather than the British spelling, for example, *civilization*, not *civilisation*.
6. Always use the preferred spelling of a word. This is the form given first in the dictionary entry.
7. Check numbers with extra care.
8. Watch for homonyms or easily confused words (for example, *their*, *there*, and *they're*; *to*, *too*, and *two*; *your* and *you're*; *its* and *it's*), as misuse can result in embarrassing errors.
9. Do not spend an inordinate amount of time debating whether compounds should be written open, hyphenated, or solid. Use your dictionary, and if the term in question is not in the dictionary, assume that it is written as an open compound (i.e., separate words).

10. Remember to paragraph for the sake of your reader. Make an effort to find suitable points at which to break up long passages.
11. Use standard proofreading symbols and use them correctly (see Illus. 10-1 and 10-2).
12. After corrections have been made, proofread to ensure that the corrections have been made properly without introducing new errors.

Miscellaneous

There are many things a CR must know and do other than those presented in this text. For example, a sound understanding of legal terminology is essential, but this is gained through courses and experience. Nonetheless, a few last-minute notes of a miscellaneous nature will be made here—in no particular order—to tie things up that may have been omitted earlier.

697 ### The CR's Worksheet

The CR should provide his/her scopist or transcriptionist with information peculiar to the transcript being prepared. This worksheet can be arranged either in alphabetical order or in order of occurrence, although many scopists and transcriptionists find an alphabetical list easier to work with. Correct spellings of persons' names are essential to the worksheet, as are other proper names, such as names of towns, companies, etc. Technical and/or medical terminology that is not general knowledge should also be included. Of course, the worksheet should state clearly the title-page information, i.e., the court and case number, etc.

698 ### Nonwords

Witnesses often mumble something that the CR should include in the transcript. Of course, the CR should not attempt to record every sound made by every witness, but certain utterances can be indicated. For example,

uh-huh (yes)	huh? (what?)
unh-unh or uh-uh (no)	

699 ### Format of a Deposition

CRs can find themselves in a variety of settings other than the courtroom; whatever the circumstances, the final product must accomplish its goal of reproducing, in written form, what was said and what trans-

Illus. 10-1   The following are proofreading symbols standard to every profession. Those that seem to have no application to the CR industry are not included here.

¶	New paragraph	∧	Caret – used to indicate where material is to be inserted or to mark the position of an error
no ¶	No new paragraph		
ℛ	Delete		
⌣	Close up		
ℛ	Delete and close up	lc	Lowercase (used in margin)
#	Insert space	/	Lowercase (used within text)
∾	Transpose		
⌐ ⌐	Center horizontally	⌐	Make all lowercase letters
⊞	Center vertically		
=	Align horizontally	Cap	Caps (used in margin)
‖	Align vertically	≡	Caps (used within text)
⊏	Move to the left		
⊐	Move to the right	⌃	Insert comma
⊓	Move up	⊙	Insert period
⊔	Move down	⌄	Insert apostrophe (or single quotation mark)
⟲	Move as shown		
⟲	Connect copy	⌄⌄	Insert quotation marks
stet	Let it stand (used in margin)	?	Insert question mark
‥‥	Let it stand (used within text)	!	Insert exclamation point
sp	Spell out the numeral or abbreviation	⊙	Insert colon
		;	Insert semicolon
		=/	Insert hyphen
		⊥/M	Insert dash
		≠ ≯	Insert parentheses
		⊏/⊐	Insert brackets

Illus. 10-2 The following passage shows
how proofreading symbols can
be used to make corrections in
your work.

When I got home, my husband and my son were scraming and

shouting, fighting over something, but I didnt know what. I heard

[their voices even before I got in the house.

I called out, Sam, Sam, What's going on in there? but noone answered

me. so I went into the house through the back and realized that they

were in the living room. I saw Sam backed up against the wall with

my husband striking at him. Sam had his hands up over his face He

was trying to protect himself from my husband's blows.

(cap)   The Court: Mrs. Freemont, could you please speak a little louder.

WITNESS: Yes, Your Honor. Sorry

THE COURT: Continue with your account, then.

Q. Your husband--is he Sam's father?

A. No. Sam's father died when Sam was just a BABY. I married

(sp) Sheperd when Sam was 12 (yrs) old.

Q. All right, Mrs. Freemont. What happened when you entered the

living room?

A. I started yelling at Sheperd to stop. *But instead of stopping, Shep* Just kept on striking out

at Sam, sometimes hitting and sometimes not. I began to pull on

Shep myself, to try to get him away from Sam, and at first he paid no

attention to me; but then he turned around and slapped me hard across my

face. *over and over* I could see that Sam was going to jump on Shep, and I was afraid

that Shep would kill my son. ~~I was right~~ *did* Sam jumped on Shep's back,

but Shep easily threw him off. *onto the floor* Sam was lying on the floor when Shep

put his boot on Sam's chest and pushed down. Sam was screaming *out* in pain.

That's when I picked up the vase and hit Shep on the head. It didn't

know *ck* him out, though, and he turned on me. He hit me repeatedly until

I could hardly see straight. In the mean time, Sam had run out of the

room and had gotten Shep's rifle. He pointed it right at Shep and said

to him--and these are his exact words--he said, "Stop hitting ma or I'll

shoot! Shep laughed and lunged at Sam. Then I heard the gun go of.

It was horrible. Sam was crying, and Shep was just lying there on

the carpet. I thought he was dead, but when I leaned over him, he

grabbed my ankel.

---

pired. There is an elastic format, seen in several variant styles from state to state, that accommodates most hearings, depositions, and other situations. The CR's employer will specify the details.

The first page of the format usually includes the name of the court, the case or docket number, the names of plaintiffs and defendants, the name of the deponent included in that particular volume, and finally the name of the CR who did the recording. Following the title sheet is usually the appearance page, on which are listed the names and addresses of all the attorneys involved in the deposition. Also included are the names of people who were present waiting to be deposed in subsequent hearings, paralegals, or perhaps third-party attorneys who play no role in that particular deposition. The next page consists of legal explanation(s) for what transpired during the deposition. Finally, the deponent is identified, and it is stated that this individual has been sworn. The questioning attorney is identified and the Q and A begins.

This is a general, loose idea of format; but it must be stressed that the CR will follow the format of his/her employer and state. There is generally a final sheet asserting the CR's impartial status.

700   Examinations

The CR should identify carefully each type of examination being conducted, e.g., Direct Examination, Cross Examination, Redirect Examination, Recross Examination, Voir Dire Examination, Rebuttal, Surrebuttal, Examination.

701   Computer-Aided Transcription

Because the computer has in its memory steno brief forms and their English equivalents, the CR can have a rough-copy transcript on which adjustments and corrections can be made before the machine prints the final copy or copies. However, the computer cannot replace the CR's need for sound grammar and punctuation skills. The CR must construct a good, accurate personal dictionary so that misspellings will not be perpetuated.

Most computer-aided transcription systems, although fast, will be faster still in the future and will demand even more sophisticated English skills from their users.

11
Cumulative Exercises

A. Correct all errors in the following:

Q. Would you state your full name for the record please?

A. Benjamin Michael O'Keefe

Q. What is your home address Sir?

A. I live at 52 Bailey Dr., Millerville Tennessee.

Q. And your age Mr. O'Keefe.

A. I'll be 80 in July, which means I'm —

Q. What is your present age?

A. 79 now.

Q. Where were you born at?

A. Brooklyn New York.

Q. Are you married?

A. I was married for thirty-nine years, but my wife her **name** was Sarah, died 5 yrs. ago.

Q. You are a widower then, is that correct?

A. Oh no, I'm married again; just last year. To this pretty young woman whose my wife now.

Q. What is your wifes name?

A. Sarah Baker O'Keefe.

Q. Your current wife's name is Sarah?

A. I'm sorry, her name is Theresa Sampson O'Keefe.

Q. Is she here? In this room today?

A. Yes. She is.

Q. Did you make a trip over seas last September?

A. Yes, I went to Ireland and Scotland.

Q. How did you travel?

A. I went with the Gate's; my friend's and neighbor's since the nineteen forties.

Q. What I meant, Mr. O'Keefe is this: By what mean's did you travel to Europe?

A. We flew. In an airplane.

Q. What was you're date of departure?

A. I left on Sept. eleventh.

Q. With which air line did you fly, do you remember?

A. I don't recall.

Q. Was this your 1st time to fly?

A. In my life time?

Q. Yes sir.

A. No—I had flown many times with my job.

Q. What kind of work do you do?

A. I don't do any thing, I've been retired now for several years.

Q. Alright. What work did you do before retirement?

A. I was an engineer with Cal-Tex International Oil Company.

Q. What is your educational back ground?

A. I have a BS Degree in structural engineering from Boston Univ.

Q. Was your wife with you on this trip last September?

A. My wife? She was with me: yes.

Q. Where in the plane were your seats?

A. Are you asking if they were first class seats?

Q. No, sir, I am asking what section of the plane were you seated. For example, in the rear, the middle, the front?

A. Oh, I see. Well I think you could say we were about mid way.

Q. You were approximately in the center section?

A. More or less.

Q. Were you seated by the window in the aisle or in a center seat?

A. I was on the aisle; and my wife was next to me.

Q. Was this the smoking or non smoking section of the plane?

A. We don't smoke.

Q. You were in the Non Smoking Section is that right?

A. That's right.

Q. Tell us how the accident occurred?

A. I got up to go to the bath room. And I was walking down the isle to go down their.

Q. And then what happened?

A. This stewardess was pushing a cart full of Soft Drinks and coffee. All of a sudden. I can't tell you why. The cart turned over. The stewardess sort of lunged forward which pushed the cart at me. The darned thing fell over on me.

Q. What were your injurys?

A. I had a broken bone in the bottom part of my leg and a bunch of bruises.

Q. Was that the extent of your injuries?

A. Some broken glass cut up my arm and face. I was sore all over.

Q. Did you see a dr. about these injurys?

A. Well sure I did.

Q. What was the name of the physician you saw, do you recall?

A. His name was Dr. Bradford.

Q. Where did you see him?

A. I saw him in his office.

Q. Where was his office?

A. I cant recall the address.

Q. Was his office some where in London?

A. That's right. After we landed in London, they took me to see Dr. Bradford.

Q. Who took you?

A. A taxi cab was arranged for me by the airline.

Q. What treatment did you receive their?

A. He set my leg in a cast.

Q. Did this Doctor Bradford do anything else for you?

A. He gave me medicine for pain.

B. The following jury charge contains a variety of errors. Find and correct all errors.

Members Of The Jury, when I have concluded my charge, I will give the case to you for determination and at that time you will take this case and you will render what ever Verdict you in your good and clear conscience and valid judgment appears to you to be the proper verdict or judgment. This trial is conducted under the laws of the state of N. Carolina and it's officials have here sought to show that under the laws of that state the accused Darnell Jarvis Morrison has violated the criminal laws there in. The defendant has pleaded not guilty to all 3 counts. I will take all three count's and explain the pertinent Laws for each. Count No. 1 allages that the defendant on the evening or night of Oct. 14, 1985 stole equipment from the office of the department of transportation. This equipment included the following items, an I.B.M. selectric III type writer, two adding machines, two tape-recorders, an electric-pencil-sharpener, and 4 boxes of computer paper. In order to convinct the defendant of those charges of theft you must be satisfied that the government has proved beyond any reasonable doubt the following elements: that, the defendent stole the goods here to fore listed, that, the defendant acted willfuly and knowingly, and with intent to de-prive the rightfull owner of these goods, that, the good's total value was over one hundred dollars. In order for goods to be stolen they must have been taken unlawfully, it does not have to be proved that the defendant intended to sell these goods however it must be proved tha possession was taken un-lawfully and with intent to deprive the owner of such possession. If you find that the goods were unlawfully removed from said Dept. of Transportation that the se goods were taken with intent to take them into his possession and for his own use whether that use be to sell or to keep then you must find a verdict of guilty. Remember that to steal something means that the defendant took possession of the stolen items having power and control over said items and this was done so unlawfully that is, contrary to the laws of this state. Ladies and gentlemen, I will not re-iterate the testimony that you have heard in this case I will instead rely on your recollection of what has been said in this court room. Remember that it is the duty of the state to prove the guilt of this and any defendant—it is not up to the defendant to prove his innocence.

C. Make corrections in the following passage.

We are here to-night to discuss the proposed new building which if constructed would be built on Gordon Rd. on 5 acres of land, now owned by a owned by Doctor and Missus Ralph Koule of Bennington, Vt. On Oct. fourth, 1986 a letter was sent to the Koule's inquiring about there possible interest in selling that parcel of land, we rec'd a reply from them on Nov. 11 stating that they would be willing to sell the land for twenty-two thousand five-hundred dollars. If we are interested the letter furter stated we should contact their attorney Mrs. Alison LeBlanc. We have contacted Mrs. LeBlanc to inform her of our possible interest and she has responded with a very general letter.

Under section VI, part B, of our by laws clearly states the procedures where by this Institution can make such land purchases. Please ladies and gentlemen turn in your copies to that section. And you will note that the procedures and guide lines are stated simply & clearly. None of these tenants as far as I can see will be violated by said proposed purchase of land. Does any one have any comment? Or disagreement?

Alright, let us continue. Section VII, part E requires that we request bids from contractor's and except the lowest one, provided that the firm offering that low bid is one of fare reputation and solid credentials. This step of course would come farther along in this process and we need not take to much time to discuss that tonight. We're all I'd imagine familiar with the process, nonetheless it must be kept in mind.

Finally, I want to remind every one here that building this proposed business center will effect the number of student's we are able too attract to this institution. We must ask ourselfs this question—are we prepared to handle an increase? How many more students are we talking about? A study will have to be made but this will take sometime but we will simply have to wait until the study is made before we can predict the affects of this proposed center.

Not since the early part of the '70's has this institution under taken such an extensive project. Its one that many want although there will be some opposition. In so far as the cost a study is all ready begun and we will have the results of the cost projections by the middle of next month.

12

Suggested References and Bibliography

There are a large number of reference books that cover various specialties, subjects that may arise in the work of a CR. The CR should be familiar with the kinds of reference materials available and be able to make use of them. No one can expect to master the peculiar jargon of every profession; that is why reference materials are so valuable. The following represents a sampling in each category, but only a sampling; there are many more available.

Suggested References

702   **Specialized Dictionaries**

Kohler's Dictionary for Accountants, ed. W.W. Cooper, Prentice-Hall.

Jane's Aerospace Dictionary, Bill Gunston, Jane's.

Dictionary of Architecture and Construction, ed. Cyril M. Harris, McGraw-Hill.

Dictionary of Business and Management, Jerry M. Rosenberg, John Wiley & Sons.

Dictionary of Computers, Data Processing, and Telecommunications, Jerry M. Rosenberg, John Wiley & Sons.

Construction Glossary: An Encyclopedic Reference and Manual, J. Stewart Stein, John Wiley & Sons.

HRC Handbook of Chemistry and Physics: A Ready Reference Book of Chemical and Physical Data, ed. Robert C. Weast, CRS Press, Inc.

McGraw-Hill Dictionary of Earth Sciences, ed. Sybil P. Parker, McGraw-Hill.

The Wiley Engineer's Desk Reference, Sanford I. Heisler, John Wiley & Sons.

McGraw-Hill Dictionary of Engineering, ed. Sybil P. Parker, McGraw-Hill.

The International Geographic Encyclopedia and Atlas, Houghton Mifflin Co.

Webster's New Geographical Dictionary, G & C Merriam Co.

Concise Dictionary of American History, Thomas C. Cochran and Wayne Andrews, Charles Scribner's Sons.

International Maritime Dictionary, Rene de Kerchove, Van Nostrand Reinhold.

Handbook of Physics and Chemistry, ed. Robert C. Weast, Chemical Rubber Co.

A Dictionary of Scientific Units, H.G. Jerrard and D.B. McNeill, Chapman and Hall.

The World Almanac and Book of Facts, Doubleday & Co. (published annually).

Columbia Lippincott Gazetteer of the World, Leon E. Seltzer, Columbia University Press.

703 Medical References

Psychiatric Dictionary, Leland E. Hinsie and Robert Jean Campbell, Oxford University Press.

Physicians' Desk Reference, Jack E. Angel, Medical Economics Co.

The Encyclopedia of Medical Tests, Cathy Pinckney and Edward Pinckney, Facts on File, Inc.

Dorland's Illustrated Medical Dictionary, W.B. Saunders Co.

Stedman's Medical Dictionary: Illustrated, ed. T.L. Stedman, Williams & Wilkins Co.

The Merck Index: An Encyclopedia of Chemicals, Drugs, and Biologicals, ed. Martha Windholz, Merck & Co.

Taber's Cyclopedic Medical Dictionary, ed. Clayton L. Thomas, F.A. Davis Co.

Human Physiology, R.F. Schmidt and G. Thews, Springer-Verlag.

704 Information on Published Materials

Books in Print: An Author-Title-Series Index to the Publishers' Trade List Annual, R. R. Bowker Co. (published annually in two volumes).

Reader's Guide to Periodical Literature, H.W. Wilson Co.

Cumulative Book Index, H.W. Wilson Co.

705 Information on People and Associations

Dictionary of National Biography, Oxford University Press.

Dictionary of American Biography, Charles Scribner's Sons.

Current Biography, H.W. Wilson Co.

Webster's Biographical Dictionary: A Dictionary of Names of Noteworthy Persons With Pronunciations and Concise Biographies, G & C Merriam Co.

Who's Who in America: A Biographical Dictionary of Notable Living Men and Women, A.N. Marquis Co. (revised and reissued biennially).
Official Congressional Directory, U.S. Government Printing Office.
Encyclopedia of Associations, Gale Research Co.

706   **Grammar and Punctuation**

The Careful Writer: A Modern Guide to English Usage, Theodore M. Bernstein, Atheneum.
A Dictionary of Modern English Usage, H.W. Fowler, Clarendon Press.
Conquer the Comma, D. Finley, GCS, Inc.
Help With the Hyphen, D. Finley, GCS, Inc.
Precision With Word Division, D. Finley, GCS, Inc.
Harbrace College Handbook, J.C. Hodges and M.E. Whitten, Harcourt Brace Jovanovich.
An English Guide for Court Reporters, Lillian Morson, Vantage Press.
English for the Shorthand Reporter, National Shorthand Reporters Association.
Writer's Guide and Index to English, Porter G. Perrin, Scott, Foresman & Co.
Practice in English, Elwood L. Prestwood, Houghton Mifflin Co.
Words Into Type, Marjorie E. Skillin, Robert M. Gay, et al., Appleton-Century-Crofts.
Grammar for Shorthand Reporters, Irwin Weiss, National Shorthand Reporters Association.
Punctuation for Shorthand Reporters, Nathaniel Weiss, National Shorthand Reporters Association.
A Manual of Style, The University of Chicago Press.
Errors in English and Ways to Correct Them, Harry Shaw, Barnes & Noble.

707   **General Dictionaries and Word Books**

20,000 Words, Louis A. Leslie, Gregg Division/McGraw-Hill.
Webster's New Dictionary of Synonyms, G & C Merriam Co.
The Complete Dictionary of Abbreviations, Robert J. Schwartz, Thomas Y. Crowell Co.
ACRONYMS, Initialisms, and Abbreviations Dictionary, ed. Ellen T. Crowley and Helen E. Sheppard, Gale Research Co.
The Random House Dictionary of the English Language, Random House.
The American Heritage Dictionary of the English Language, American Heritage Publishing Co. and Houghton Mifflin Co.
The American College Dictionary, Random House.

Webster's Third New International Dictionary of the English Language, Unabridged, G & C Merriam Co.

Webster's New World Dictionary of the American Language, William Collins Publishers.

Webster's Ninth New Collegiate Dictionary, Merriam-Webster.

708   Legal Terminology

Black's Law Dictionary, Henry C. Black, West Publishing Co.

Stroud's Judicial Dictionary of Words and Phrases, John S. James, Sweet and Maxwell, Ltd.

Legal Studies, to Wit: Basic Legal Terminology and Transcription, Wanda Walker Roderick, South-Western Publishing Co.

Bibliography

Finley, D. *Conquer the Comma!* Lake Park, Florida: GCS, Inc., 1978.

_____. *Help With the Hyphen.* Lake Park, Florida: GCS, Inc., 1978.

_____. *Precision With Word Division.* Lake Park, Florida: GCS, Inc., 1978.

Freer, Carolee. *Computer Shorthand: Speed Building and Transcription.* New York: John Wiley & Sons, 1984.

French, Christopher W., Eileen A. Powell, and Howard Angione (eds.). *The Associated Press Stylebook and Libel Manual.* Reading, Massachusetts: Addison-Wesley Publishing Co., 1980.

Gordon, Frank S., Thomas M.S. Hemnes, and Charles E. Weinstein. *The Legal Word Book,* 2d ed. Boston: Houghton Mifflin Co., 1982.

Hodges, J.C., and M.E. Whitten. *Harbrace College Handbook,* 9th ed. New York: Harcourt Brace Jovanovich, 1982.

Lidell, Theo C. *Basic Language: Messages and Meanings.* New York: Harper & Row, 1983.

Morson, Lillian I. *An English Guide for Court Reporters.* New York: Vantage Press, 1974.

National Shorthand Reporters Association. *English for the Shorthand Reporter.* Vienna, Virginia: National Shorthand Reporters Association, 1975.

Perry, Devern. *College Vocabulary Building,* 7th ed. Cincinnati: South-Western Publishing Co., 1983.

_____, and J.E. Silverthorn. *Word Division Manual,* 3d ed. Cincinnati: South-Western Publishing Co., 1984.

Prestwood, Elwood L., and Bertha Handlan Campbell. *Practice in English.* Boston: Houghton Mifflin Co., 1979.

Sachs, H.J., H.M. Brown, and P.J. Canavan. *Practical English Workbook*. New York: D. Van Nostrand Company, 1978.

Shaw, Harry. *Errors in English and Ways to Correct Them*, 2d ed. New York: Barnes & Noble, 1970.

The University of Chicago Press. *A Manual of Style*, 12th ed. Chicago: University of Chicago Press, 1969.

Webster's Ninth New Collegiate Dictionary. Springfield, Massachusetts: Merriam-Webster, 1985.

Weiss, Irwin. *Grammar for Shorthand Reporters*. Vienna, Virginia: National Shorthand Reporters Association, 1978.

Weiss, Nathaniel. *Punctuation for Shorthand Reporters*. Vienna, Virginia: National Shorthand Reporters Association, 1971.

Index

Numbers refer to paragraph numbers.

Numbers refer to paragraph numbers.

Numbers refer to paragraph numbers.

Numbers refer to paragraph numbers.

Numbers refer to paragraph numbers.

Q

R

Numbers refer to paragraph numbers.

Numbers refer to paragraph numbers.

Notes

Notes _____

Notes